The Upanishads & Life

The Upanishads & Life

W.S. URQUHART

GYAN PUBLISHING HOUSE
New Delhi - 110002

The Upanishads & Life

ISBN : 9788121200486

Rs. 480

Reprinted 2016 in India by
Gyan Publishing House
5 , Main Ansari Road, Daryaganj,
New Delhi - 110002
Phones : 9811692060

E-mail : books@gyanbooks.com
gyanbook@vsnl.com
Website: gyanbooks.com

TO MY

FATHER AND MOTHER

CONTENTS

CHAP.		PAGE
I.	THE SETTING OF THE PROBLEM OF THE UPANISHADS	1
II.	THE GENERAL CHARACTER OF THE SOLUTION.	25
III.	THE PANTHEISM AND PESSIMISM OF THE SYSTEM	49
IV.	THE INTELLECTUALISM OF THE UPANISHADS AND THEIR METAPHYSICAL INADEQUACY ...	74
V.	THE RELIGIOUS AND ETHICAL EFFECTS ...	99
VI.	THE NEED OF THEISM AND THE MESSAGE OF CHRISTIANITY	126

PREFACE

EVEN the slightest study of Indian philosophy reveals the central place which the Upanishads hold both in the thought of former days and at the present time. I have endeavoured in this volume to examine and appreciate the leading conceptions of the Upanishads, but my main purpose has been the more practical one of attempting to establish a relation between these conceptions and the life of the people. It seems to me that the admiration so fittingly given to these great legacies of the past, will be bestowed with more real discrimination, and have more real value, if the ideas of the Upanishads are brought to the test of application to present-day religious, ethical and social problems. Amongst a people with whom the intellectual tradition is so strong as in India, every great movement must have a thought-basis, and my task has been to discover whether the Upanishads can supply an adequate basis of this nature. The conclusion which I have reached is that a certain amount of transformation of the ancient ideas is necessary, if India is to find sufficient intellectual support for the progress which is even now being made in matters relating to religion and ethics, and I hope that those who do not quite approve of this somewhat critical attitude, will do me the justice of believing that it has been reached after an honest attempt to carry a sympathetic and unprejudiced spirit into my investigation. Those who care to pursue the argument of the present volume further will find it partially incorporated in a larger work, entitled *Pantheism and the Value of Life—with special reference to Indian Philosophy*, which I wrote as a thesis for the degree of Doctor of Philosophy, and which will shortly be published.

The present book was arranged for some years ago, but various causes have led to delay in publication. I have to express my indebtedness to Dr. J. N. Farquhar for several valuable suggestions. In the revision of the proofs, also, I have received much assistance from him and from my wife.

Scottish Churches College,
Calcutta, 1916.

W. S. URQUHART.

THE UPANISHADS AND LIFE

CHAPTER I

The Setting of the Problem of the Upanishads

IT is a justifiable demand that any system of religion or philosophy should enable us to take up a definite attitude to the practical concerns of life. It must involve certain judgments as to the relative values of objects, and must guide us in our relations to them. It must assign some reasons for calling them either good or bad, and thus influence our conduct in regard to them. To ignore such a demand would confine philosophy within the limits of a merely intellectual discipline, and would give point to the objection that the study of it is an altogether unprofitable employment of the powers of the human mind. Least of all can such a demand be ignored in connection with the thought of India, where philosophy has always tended to pass into religion and has been regarded as affording some kind of solution of the pressing problems of life.

The aim of the present volume is to examine the fundamental doctrines of Indian philosophy, as these are indicated in the Upanishads—the chief storehouse for Indian philosophical thought—and to estimate the effect which such doctrines may be expected to have upon our practical attitude to life. The influence of these books will be found to be part of the larger question of the influence of all pantheistic thought, especially of an idealistic character, upon our sense of the value of life. And it is an influence which is by no means confined within the uncertain boundaries of the period during which these books were composed, but one which continues down to the present day and still determines fundamentally the thought and conduct of the India in which we live.

It is becoming increasingly natural to turn to India for material illustrative of philosophical problems. Three-quarters of a century ago Cousin wrote, "We are constrained to bow the knee to the philosophy of the East, and to see in the cradle of the human race the native land of the highest philosophy." On all hands the greatness of India's heritage of philosophic thought is being recognised, and vigorous efforts are being made to remove the barriers which centuries of differing custom and environment have placed between the Eastern and the Western mind. "*Ex oriente lux*" has become more than a meaningless motto, even though for the Western enquirer clouds of obscurity may still hang low over the eastern horizon.

For those who are interested especially in the study of pantheistic types of thought, Indian philosophy offers its peculiar attractions, for here we have, as we shall see, pantheism in its purest form. In the thought of other lands pantheism has, no doubt, been a constantly recurring tendency, but sometimes long periods have elapsed between its appearances, and, when it emerges it has to struggle with opponents and often yield the victory to them. In India there was struggle also, but it was not a struggle between equals. Pantheism secured and retained predominance with comparative ease, and such terms as had to be made were wholly in its favour. In any case the conflict was rather with popular beliefs than with other fully developed systems of philosophical thought. Thus the study of pantheism in India is not complicated so much as in other lands by the necessity of taking account of conflicting tendencies, and the intellectual inheritance of the past is the most important influence at the present day. The most popular books are those in which the pantheistic strain is unmistakeable. The religion of the vast majority of the educated classes is a refined pantheism, and toward the popular religion they adopt that attitude of welcome to all forms, and indifference to any particular form, which pantheism specially encourages. Even the illiterate classes, in their occasional reflective moods, allow their thoughts to run upon pantheistic lines. From its cradle onwards to the present day the thought of India has been " radically pantheistic."

The comparative freedom of Indian pantheism from disturbing influences undoubtedly simplifies the problem of estimating its effects, but at the same time this isolation creates new difficulties. For the Indian student pantheism is like the atmosphere—the very universality of its pressure makes him unconscious of it. It is impossible for him to get outside the range of its influence and occupy the detached position which is necessary for unbiassed estimation of its value. Of course, esoteric criticism has its compensations in the way of sympathy and intuitive understanding, but there is also danger that disabilities which are in reality serious defects, may be regarded as of little account, or taken as a matter of course—and in either case removed from the sphere of criticism.

For the student who approaches Indian pantheism from the standpoint of a different tradition, there are just the opposite difficulties. By those who sympathise without understanding he will be told that he understands without sympathising, and that therefore he cannot really understand. Difficulties, which would be no difficulties to the student of Indian nationality, will confront him. The philosophical truth in the ancient books will often seem to be hidden under a mass of verbiage, mythology and obsolete ceremonial injunction. To a certain extent the Eastern scholar would sympathise, but would not appreciate the full meaning of the difficulty. For him these wrappings of the thought would be symbols of a spirit which he still cherished, though he might now express it differently. He would be able to trace the ceremonial rites back to their origin, and would understand that then they had a meaning not altogether to be despised. Seemingly fantastic phraseology would help him to discover the truth instead of concealing it.

An illustration of the difficulties which confront those of us who approach Indian thought from the outside may be found in the frequency of the injunction to meditate upon the syllable *Om*. At first this appears to be an unmeaning absurdity, but, as we reflect, we discover that we have here a symbol indicative of a whole point of view and inciting to varied philosophical reflection. Not only does the syllable represent reflection upon the Vedas: it stands as a symbol of speech and life. In reflecting upon it we discover that we are reflecting upon the soul of man and realising our unity with the soul of nature. Throughout its uses the syllable indicates a concentration of thought to which we are unaccustomed, and to which we find it difficult to attain. The Chhandogya Upanishad, *e.g.*, opens with the injunction, "Let a man meditate on the syllable *Om*," and at first we may be disposed to find little meaning in this. But further reflection will show us that we have here a compendious formula capable of application throughout the major portions of Indian philosophy. As Max Müller says, "It is a mistake to conclude that we have here '*vox et praeterea nihil*.' Meditation on the syllable *Om* consisted in long continued repetition of that syllable, with a view of drawing the thoughts away from all other subjects and concentrating them on some higher object of thought, of which that syllable was made to be the symbol. This concentration of thought, *ekagratā*, or one-pointedness, as the Hindus call it, is something to us almost unknown. Our minds are like kaleidoscopes of thoughts in constant motion, and to shut our mental eye to everything else, while dwelling on one thought only, has become to most of us almost as impossible as to apprehend one musical note without harmonics. With the life we are leading now—with telegrams, letters, newspapers, reviews, pamphlets and books ever breaking in upon us—it has become impossible, or almost impossible, ever to arrive at that intensity of thought which the Hindu meant by *ekagratā*, and the attainment of which was to them the indispensable condition of all philosophical and religious speculation."[1]

The impossibility, or at least the difficulty, of attaining the Indian point of view, which arises from the complexity of our modern civilisation and its many occupations, is not the whole of the matter. We also differ in our estimation of the value of this point of view.

Our conception of knowledge is different. The Indian mind leans to the intuitive, the Western to the discursive and empirical. The Indian emphasises intensity of knowledge; the Western extensity. It might even be said that the Indian mind is more naturally philosophical and the Western more naturally scientific, were it not that this would introduce a false contrast between philosophy and science. But there is at least a partial truth in the following description of the contrast given by a modern novelist, though we do not follow him in the limitations which he assigns to the Western philosophical attitude. "In India there prevails an idea that knowledge can be assimilated once for all, that if you can obtain it, you immediately possess the knowledge of everything, the pass-key that shall unlock every door. That is the reason of the prolonged fasting and solitary meditation of the ascetics. They believe that by attenuating the bond between soul and body, the soul can be liberated and can temporarily identify itself with other objects, animate and inanimate, besides the especial body to which it belongs, and they believe that this direct knowledge remains. Western philosophers argue that the only acquaintance a man can have with bodies external to his mind is that which he acquires by the medium of his bodily senses—though these are external to the mind in the truest sense."[2]

This *one-pointedness* of the Indian attitude is a source of many other differences which we need not enter into here, but which will emerge in the course of our discussion. It explains, amongst other things, the peculiarly idealistic character of Indian pantheism, and

---

[1] *Sacred Books of the East*, Vol. I, p. 24.

[2] Marion Crawford, *Mr. Isaacs*.

the prevalent readiness to sacrifice the multiplicity of the world. It may explain also the tendency towards passivity rather than activity, the slight emphasis upon personality, and the transcendence of distinctions in the moral sphere which to the Western mind seem fundamental. The differences between the two points of view are important, and must not be forgotten. They render our task difficult but not impossible, for, after all, there is a unity in all activity of the human mind, deeper than all differences of race and time.

The *Upanishads* may be taken as typical of, and to a large extent responsible for, the pantheistic tendency we have noted as the prevailing characteristic of Indian thought. But, before proceeding to an examination of their doctrines, we must attempt, however briefly, to indicate their place in Indian literary history, and also to indicate the form in which they received the particular problems of human life with which they were called upon to deal.

The chronology of the various books and, indeed, of the systems of philosophy they indicate, is an almost insoluble problem. We have to deal to a very large extent with oral tradition rather than with written documents, and a comparative lack of historical sense has suffered many important data to pass into oblivion. The establishment of any detailed chronology is therefore out of the question; indeed the dates in Indian literary history have been compared to nine-pins, which are set up only to be knocked down again.

The *Upanishads* form the main part of the system of the *Vedanta*, which includes, besides the *Upanishads*, the Sutras derived from them in the course of centuries of development, as well as the Commentaries of Sankara and Ramanuja. Though our study will lie almost entirely within this group, it may be useful to place it within a still larger group, as there are unmistakeable prophecies in the *Vedas* of the doctrines with which we have to deal, and there is also a vast body of contemporaneous and subsequent literature which has been affected by them.

Attempts have been made to trace a line of demarcation between an old Vedic period (to which the *Rig-Veda* at least belongs) and a new Vedic period, containing the rest of the Vedic literature with the Brahmanas and the Upanishads. The year 1000 B.C. has been chosen as roughly indicating a line of division, and the length of the second period has been calculated at about 500 years. It is most probable, however, that certain portions of the *Atharva Veda* should be reckoned as belonging to the same period as the *Rig-Veda*. Other writers on the subject would make the division into three periods, closing the Vedic period at about 1300 B.C., and inserting thereafter a Brahmanic or Sacerdotal period, lasting till about 600 B.C. The properly Philosophic period would, according to both these views, begin with the composition of the *Upanishads*, approximately about the sixth century B.C. Others again would push back the composition of the *Upanishads* to the ninth century, and thus unite it much more closely with the period of Brahmanic development. The Chhandogya and Brihadaranyaka Upanishads at least show characteristics which connect them very closely with the *Rig-Veda*. No attempt to assign more definite chronology has, however, succeeded, and we find that the periods selected are constantly changing their boundaries and overlapping one another. All that can be said is that the main direction is from the *Rig-Veda* to the other *Vedas*, from *Vedic* literature as a whole to the *Brahmanas*, and from these, again, through the *Aranyakas* to the *Upanishads*. We should remember, however, that portions of the *Atharva Veda* are contemporaneous with the *Rig-Veda*, that some of the earliest *Upanishads* are not much later than the latest *Vedas*, and that some of the *Brahmanas*, at least, are subsequent to some of the *Upanishads*.

The *Rig-Veda* is the oldest of the Vedas and consists of hymns to the gods, hymns remarkable at once for their antiquity and their beauty, and intended to be used by the *hotri* or first order of priests. The

Sama-Veda is derived almost entirely from the *Rig-Veda.* It is a manual intended for use by the second order of priests, chiefly at the time of the *Soma* sacrifice. The verses were sung to certain fixed tunes, so that the collection may be described as a book of chants. The name given to the second order of priest, *Udgatri*, signifies, literally, singer. The *Yajur-Veda* consisted partly of verse formulas and partly of prose, and was designed for use at the various sacrifices. At a late date the verse portions were separated from the prose, and we thus obtain two forms of the *Yajur-Veda*, the older or mixed edition being called the *Black Yajur-Veda*, and the unmixed being called the *White Yajur-Veda.* Certain portions of the *Atharva Veda* are, in the opinion of many writers, *e.g.*, Oldenberg, of equal antiquity with the *Rig-Veda*, but to a large extent it was much later than the other *Vedas*, and only gradually acquired equal importance with them. It differs considerably from the other Vedas. Its outlook on life is on the whole more gloomy, and it is greatly influenced by magical and superstitious ideas which had crept in from lower strata of the population. The *Brahmanas* were ritual text-books used in connection with the *Samhitas*, or collections of verses, belonging to the ancient Vedas. These Brahmanas belong to a later age, when the creative impulse had largely disappeared and reverence for tradition had taken its place. It was necessary for the priests of each class to learn by heart the Veda of his order, and, further, to apply it to the details of an ever-growing ceremonial. Codes of instruction were thus required which would embody the sacerdotal traditions and the various interpretations of the Vedic originals, and also guide the priest through the complexities of the ritual. Differences of detail in interpretation, and in ritual practice, led to the formation of various schools, or *S'ākhās*, each with their own Brahmana, but united in the common task of applying the Vedic text to purposes of ritual and worship. We have thus not only Brahmanas containing instruction for each class of priests, but also Brahmanas representing differences within these classes.

An external cause led to further literary modification. The third stage of the ideal life was held to be that of the *Vanaprastha*, or dweller in the woods, who, after having fulfilled the duties of a householder, betook himself to the forests for meditation. Such a recluse could find no use for the details of ritual observance. He might, however, retain the essential value of the interpretation in such form as could be meditated upon in the depths of the forest. To meet such a need the *Aranyakas* were composed. They have been described as "*Brahmanas* appointed for the vow of an anchorite," and they contained the ritual and the allegorical teaching which would form a suitable preparation for the hermit life. They form the link between the *Brahmanas* and the *Upanishads*.

A still higher condition of life than that of the *Vanaprastha* may be vaguely distinguished. The life of the recluse, when extended to extreme old age, was supposed to culminate in freedom from all desires and from all duties, his wandering and homeless life being symbolical of the attainment of such practical abstraction. The *Upanishads*, which form the concluding portions of the *Aranyakas*, correspond, in the sphere of thought, to this concluding stage of actual life. They contain the essential doctrines in which the ritual of the *Brahmanas* and the theosophical interpretations of the *Aranyakas* were supposed to find their culmination.

"How entirely does the Oupnekhat breathe throughout the holy spirit of the Vedas," ejaculates Schopenhauer, and he is to a certain extent justified, for the *Upanishads* may be regarded as spiritually the successors of the *Vedas*. They are not properly philosophical treatises, but they are the source from which the main stream of Indian philosophy has flowed, and in particular they are constitutive of the Vedanta. It is impossible to fix the dates of their composition, and conjectures vary to the extent of six hundred years and more, *i.e.*, from 1000 B.C. to 400 B.C., and some, *e.g.*, the

Svetasvatara, may be considerably later even than this. Their composition extended over many centuries, and the form in which they now appear is the resultant of many previous forms. The Upanishads of the three older Vedas were very closely connected with the schools attached to these Vedas, and indeed took their names from the names of the schools. The Upanishads of the *Atharva Veda* were neither so connected nor so named, and the canon was much more open. Any later statement of mystical doctrine whatsoever was assigned to the *Atharva Veda*.

Tradition points to an enormous number of Upanishads. As many as 230 are said, *e.g.*, by Weber, to have been at one time in existence, but for this total there is little authority. Eleven Upanishads are commented on by Sankara, and these may be taken as the most important, and to a certain extent fixed the canon. These are distributed amongst the Vedas as follows:—

Rig-Veda—Aitareya.
Sama-Veda—Chhandogya and Kena.
Yajur (Black)—Taittiriya, Katha, and Svetasvatara.
Yajur (White)– Isa and Brihadaranyaka.
Atharva Veda—Mundaka, Prasna, and Mandukya.

To these eleven may be added the Kaushitaki, belonging to the Rig-Veda; the Mahanarayana and the Maitrayaniya, belonging to the Black Yajur Veda. The eleven commented on by Sankara may again be divided into major and minor. To the major class belong the Chhandogya and the Briha. These two are also probably older than the others. In them no work belonging to post-Vedic times is referred to, and, as already pointed out, they contain certain qualities which connect them very closely with the Rig-Veda. Of the minor Upanishads the Svetasvatara is sometimes regarded as later than many of the others, and between them and it a development, both circumstantial and doctrinal, has been traced.

The central teaching of the Upanishads seems to find more acceptance amongst the *Kshatriyas* at the period of the older Upanishads, while in the later

Upanishads the positions are reversed, and the Brahmins appear to be supreme. We may also notice a growing fixity of caste and a greater prevalence of ascetic practices. In doctrine the pantheism of the system has become more pronounced by the time the Upanishads of the *Atharva Veda* are composed. The *Svetasvatara* Upanishad has often been taken to be a work of later date, because of its references to well-established schools of philosophy and its alleged sectarian tendencies. The evidence for a considerably later date does not, however, appear to be conclusive, and the modifications of the doctrine of the older Upanishads, which it introduces, do not require any great length of time for their development. R. C. Bose, in his *Hindu Philosophy*, enphasises the late character of this Upanishad, but bothMax Müller and Deussen regard the evidence as inconclusive.

Before referring to the present-day importance of the Upänishads, we may trace briefly the subsequent development of Vedantic literature. The next stage is to be found in the *Vedanta Sutras*, which represent the culmination of a number of tentative efforts to put the teaching of the *Upanishads* in a more or less literary and philosophical form. The *Sutras*, as Dr. Thibaut says, "combine the two tasks of concisely stating the doctrine of the Upanishads and of argumentatively establishing the special interpretation of the Vedas adopted in the Sutras."[1] The main body of Sutras (called *Vedanta*, *Sariraka* or *Brahma Sutras*) is attributed to Badarayana or Vyasa. The mass of material which the priests had by this time to deal with had become unmanageable, and the Sutras aim, above all, at brevity. To this desire for brevity they often sacrificed intelligibility. As Professor Macdonell says, "The prose in which these works are composed is so compressed that the wording of the most laconic telegram would appear diffuse compared with it."[2] The composers of some of the Sutras are said to delight as much in the saving of a short vowel as in the birth of son. The result of all

---

[1] *Sacred Books of the East*, Vol. XXXIV, p. 12.
[2] *Sanskrit Literature*, p. 36.

this is that the Sutras are almost unintelligible without commentaries, and their importance is largely absorbed in that of the great commentaries which have been devoted to their exposition. For one of these commentaries Sankara, who flourished in the ninth century, was responsible, and another is the work of Ramanuja, who belongs to the twelfth century. Sankara is usually taken to be the most orthodox exponent of the Upanishad doctrine which has been handed down through the Sutras, and his interpretation has dominated the subsequent course of the Vedanta philosophy. It is, however, a matter of controversy whether on all points he correctly represented the doctrine, or whether he must not occasionally give place to Ramanuja.

The great commentaries of Sankara, Ramanuja and Madhvacharyya, etc., practically close the authoritative literature of the Vedanta. A certain indication of the relation of the three parts of the literature to one another is given by the comparison of the *Upanishads* to the Gospels, the Sutras to the Epistles, and the works of Sankara and Ramanuja, etc., to outstanding New Testament commentaries. It may be pointed out also that the influence of the Upanishads, and of the philosophy which they represent, is to be traced in certain side currents and in literature which is not primarily philosophical. The spirit of the philosophy reappears in the *Laws of Manu*, one of the oldest of the post-Vedic books, which did not, however, assume its present form until shortly before the Christian era, or perhaps not much earlier even than 200 A.D. The *Gita*, more especially in its second part, breathes the same spirit, and manifests many resemblances to the *Upanishads*, particularly to the *Svetasvatara*.[1] The religion of the *Puranas* (dating roughly from the sixth to the twelfth centuries A.D.) is essentially pantheistic in its tendency, and it is a pantheism which is specifically used as a basis for popular polytheism and a justification of it. All modern literature dealing with religious and philosophical topics is profoundly influenced by the Upanishads. Indeed, it

---

[1] Cf. *Gita*, 9-27, 8-9, 7-7, 13-17.

might be said that Indian literature in general is coloured by their thought, and the popular religions draw their inspiration from them. Barth notes the width of their influence, and shows that from them support has been drawn even for less desirable forms of popular religion. "The less religious will borrow from them the externals of devotion: the baser sort and the more worthless will wrap themselves up in their mysticism and appropriate their formula. It is with the word Brahman and deliverance on his lips that the alchemist will form to himself a religion of his search for the philosopher's stone, that the votaries of Kali will slaughter their victims, and certain of the Sivaites give themselves over to their riotous revels."[1]

Their influence upon the more elevated forms of religion is still more obvious. Sometimes this influence works by way of unconscious inheritance, but very frequently religious leaders of modern time give definite expression to their sense of indebtedness to the *Upanishads*. They are not regarded as properly formulated philosophical treatises, but rather, as Barth puts it, as "pre-eminently exhortations to the spiritual life." Rajah Ram Mohan Roy, the religious reformer of the nineteenth century, expressed the belief that "if a selection were made from the Upanishads, it would contribute more than any other publication to the religious improvement of the people." He put them on a level far above other religious literature, and, in Max Müller's words, "regarded them as something different from all the rest, something that should not be thrown away, something that, if rightly understood, might supply the right native soil in which alone the seeds of true religion, aye, of true Christianity, might spring up again and prosper in India."[2] One of the more recent Brahmo leaders, the Rev. P. C. Mazumdar, refers to them in the following terms of profound appreciation: "The sublime self-assertion of the Upanishads, the rapt mind beholding the spirit of

---

[1] *Religions of India*, p. 84.
[2] *Sacred Books*, Vol. VIII, p. 63.

all things in itself, the secret of the whole universe revealed within the soul, the heaven of heavens in the earth, the fire that kindles all fire, the life that breathes itself into all existence, tend to create a glorious idealism before which the hard and hardening world of matter hides its diminished head."[1] Their normative character for all thought is thus indicated by Professor Dutt Shastri, in the book he has just published on the *Doctrine of Maya*, "They are canonical, and quotations from them are held by tradition complete and self-sufficient and require no further support. They are final authorities."[2]

Having shown the place which the Upanishads hold in Indian literary history, and the extent of their present-day influence, we may devote the remainder of this chapter to an attempt to indicate the form in which they received their main problems. By the time Indian thought becomes susceptible of philosophical treatment, as it is in the Upanishads, it is regarded as the answer to profound spiritual questionings on the part of those in whom a full sense of the gravity of the problems had been developed. Indeed, the gravity might be described as excessive. The background is pessimistic, and the solution sought for is of the nature of a remedy rather than a mere play of unpractical speculation. Men desire, and desire with the passionateness of religious yearning, a deliverance from sorrow rather than an enhancement of their joys.

Now this attitude presents a striking contrast to early Vedic religion. The religion of the Vedas is, for the most part, a religion of joy, an expression of delight at being alive in a great and glorious world. The impressive phases of nature are taken as the objects of religious worship—centres about which the mythological fancy may group legends of awe-inspiring but not terrifying nature. For the most part it is the benignant aspects of the powers and process of nature which occupy the mind of the worshipper, though, of course,

---

[1] *Rise and Progress of the Brahmo Samaj*, p. 129.

[2] *Ibid.*, p. 48.

traces of fear may also be noted, due to the persistence of the earlier animistic beliefs in demons and lesser gods. The attitude towards the gods is on the whole one of joyous trust. The gods can be kept in good humour by sacrifice; they are interested in all the particular concerns of their worshippers, and sharers even in their social joys. Sometimes, indeed, they show a certain amount of jealousy of mortals, but, in the main, they are well disposed and under their benign rule men may live a life of innocence and brightness, a life dominated by easily satisfied materialistic desires for health, wealth, and protection against enemies. Yet the gladness is superficial, and is the result of unconsciousness and of innocence rather than of struggle. It is possible only through an avoidance of the truly spiritual quest. It represents a victory over primitive fears of demons, through the imagination of beneficent deities more powerful still. It is the gladness of a child, who, in the light of the morning and in the presence of protecting friends, forgets the terrors of the darkness, and for whom questions as to the permanence of the light and the power of its protectors have not yet arisen. There is no great development of the moral sense. In the most of the hymns, with the exception of some addressed to Varuna, the deepest moral fault is omission or error in sacrificial ceremony, by which the benefit expected may be prevented from reaching the worshipper. At the best the world of the age of the *Rig-Veda* is but "halfway to morality," and the sense of light-hearted joyousness is maintained only through unconsciousness of the deeper problems of thought and life. The sins of which the worshippers of Varuna are conscious are sins of error and of ignorance rather than of wilfulness, and their cry is for mercy rather than for forgiveness, a prayer that the error should be overlooked, because it is only an error and nothing more, rather than a sense of shame born of true ethical repentance. It is also rather a race consciousness of sin than an individual consciousness. For these reasons it did not carry its own healing with it, and thus, while it indicated a present mood of insufficient seriousness, was not able to prevent a subsequent reaction towards a darker view of life.

In order to understand such a reaction, we must refer to certain tendencies which are implicit in Vedic thought, and the outcome of which was a growing sense of the helplessness and insignificance of the individual, and of the poverty and wretchedness of his life in the presence of universal forces. The Hindu mind has repeatedly travelled along the path that leads from polytheism to pantheism, and had begun to do so even in Vedic times. There is a dawning consciousness that above the popular gods there is one eternal and unfathomable unity. It was a development curiously similar to that which took place in Greece in the transition from the point of view of the Homeric epics to the idealistic schools of philosophers, such as the Eleatics. Slowly and steadily the philosophic leaven worked. At first men seemed almost afraid of it, and the doctrine of the "secret names" of the gods points to an esoteric doctrine which was too great a mystery to be revealed to the vulgar.

The progress towards unity is aided by certain characteristics of the Vedic popular religion. Only a slight degree of personification is applied to the Vedic deities. They are often little more than names of natural processes, and the same natural process may have several names associated with it. The functions of the gods are thus easily interchangeable, and the next step is that instead of different gods representing different qualities, the qualities are combined, and, by a process of generalisation, one god is taken to represent a very considerable group. The gods having been found to possess common qualities, it is then easy to substantialize the common qualities and declare that the gods are one in essence. One god may be found to be the most complete embodiment of this essence and to be worthy therefore of supreme regard. This "essential god" may then be regarded as the ground or source out of which the other gods emerged. As illustrating this process, we may compare the formula, "Agni is all the gods." Hunt thus describes the transition: "Every deity is in the first instance a natural object; it is then invested with all the powers in nature; it has ascribed to it all the qualities of all things cognisable by the senses, and thus it becomes the supreme god, constituting the all of nature."[1]

The position reached has been described as Henotheism, by which is meant a system of belief under which a god is, for the time being, arbitrarily taken as supreme, whereas at another time and in another place another god may receive this honour. Barth urges that within the period we are considering it is impossible to get beyond this position, but it may be questioned whether such a shifting pantheon is ultimately satisfying even to the composers of the Vedas. Their speculative genius points in the direction of a more permanent unity, not perhaps explicitly stated or indicated by an undetachable name, but conceived of as the goal of thought. We may, however, agree with Barth in holding that there is no permanent hierarchy, and may add that the tendency is rather towards monism than towards monotheism.

There are various other indications of the process towards unity. The gods are arranged, *e.g.*, in pairs and trinities. We have the primal Dyaus and Prithivi, and the trinity of Surya, Indra and Agni, whom Yaska, about 500 B.C. takes to be representative of the whole Vedic pantheon. There is also the grouping of gods according to locality, as the gods of the sky, the air, and the earth. In the third hymn of the first book we meet with the curious conception of *Visve devas*, or all-gods. This may mean a special group of gods, or all the gods together, or, according to some authorities, the conception is a priestly manufacture securing that none of the gods will be omitted in laudations expressly intended for all the gods. Any of these interpretations, however, witnesses to a primitive mental effort, always struggling against diversity, to express the unity of the forces on which ultimately men depend.

[1] *Pantheism*, p. 6.

The physical universality of the objects worshipped also assist in the progress towards a pantheistic unity. Especially are the gods of the sky and the air combined so as to produce an impression of spatial immensity, overshadowing, all-embracing, and all-pervading. *Aditi* typifies an overshadowing material infinity, and the air is all-pervading, reaching as one universal element to the corners of the world.

The attempts at creative explanation also show the prevalence of the idea of an all-inclusive and all-productive substance. The conception of *Purusha* is that of one substance from which all things in the world are produced. We may trace the development from material to efficient cause through the conceptions of Prajapati, Visvakarman, Hiranyagarbha, and Viraj, noting a gradual advance from the grossly material and passive to the semi-spiritual and active, and an ever more successful effort to reduce the materials and forces of the world to one single all-embracing explanation.

For the purposes of our special problem, *viz.*, the causes of the disappearance of the joyous spirit, it should be remembered that the popularity of a god does not increase with the increase of his dignity. The tendency is rather in the opposite direction. For popularity a god must be the embodiment of some near physical force or be invested with characteristics akin to those of concrete human personality. As a god attains the universality which appeals to the philosopher and the mystic, he loses part of his influence over the masses.

More generally it may be said that as the number of the gods decreased, and the feeling of their immensity and overpowering might increased, contrasts began to make themselves felt between human life and the realities which lay darkly hidden behind these circumstances. The growing consciousness of unity and the manifestations of it, threw into stronger relief the diversities and confusions of human nature. Human vexations might, indeed, appear to be trifling, but this would not be the immediate result. The first effect of the contrast would be to increase the sense of the intolerableness of life. Men become more acutely conscious of the imperfections of their life when they have some great conception wherewith they may contrast these imperfections.

For the less speculative minds it would appear that the gods were being removed to a greater distance from them. They were no longer the homely familiar deities, capturing the popular fancy. Thus the world became comparatively void to the ordinary worshipper. He was left with only a few somewhat uninteresting deities, while doubts were cast upon the value of the gods towards which his devotion would naturally go forth. Further, the physical universality of the objects of worship which, as we have seen, assisted the minds of the worshippers in their search after unity, and gave substantiality and support to their general conceptions, became through this very search emphasised, the result being that the more awe-inspiring characters of even the popular gods overshadowed those which might otherwise have evoked confidence, and deepened the contrast between the immensity of divinity and the little lives of men. The sky was the all-embracing, the air was the all-pervading, and the sun was the light before which all other lights grew dim. And, moreover, the sky, the air and the sun were permanent, and made men feel more than ever that they themselves were only the children of a day.

The influence of these conceptions would probably disturb the somewhat easy-going satisfaction with materialistic happiness to which we have referred. We find in place of it an upward tendency, and a yearning after, and appreciation of spiritual satisfaction. But spiritual satisfaction cannot be so easily obtained as material satisfaction, and thus the first result of dissatisfaction with the material will meet with no immediate compensation from the spiritual sphere.

Attempts also at the explanation of evil have, as their first effect, disturbance rather than relief. In primitive polytheism the explanation of evil lies near at hand. It is due to demons, who are indeed powerful, but who may be overcome by still more powerful gods. But the emergence of the conception of unity makes it necessary to trace evil back to a universal cause. Evil thus becomes a burden from which there is no relief, because it is bound up with the reality of the universal cause, and shares in a world necessity.

And this burden of evil is the more depressing because it is not properly recognised as evil. It is vaguely conceived as a grim oppressive reality, and thus there is no "thinking through" to an adequate solution. The reason of this failure to recognise the true nature of evil lies in the slightly developed sense of ethical responsibility, which prevents the connection between the human will and evil. We are thus unable to regard evil as intelligible and removable by human activity. The incidence of pain and misery on human life must then be attributed entirely to the universal cause, and the result is a feeling of helplessness and a sense of injustice.

The reconciliation between man and God, through a sense of spiritual kinship which would bring courage and strength, is further prevented by the persistence of ideas borrowed from a lower stratum of belief. The idea of magic is by no means absent from the Vedas, and it is an idea which is associated with priestcraft and the degradation of the worshipper. Although the idea of unity has been reached, the hidden force of the world is still regarded as a fluid and semi-material reality, which the worshipper, by means of certain rites and incantations, may participate in, and thus obtain divine power by what is very like a process of physical assimilation. This lower idea is perhaps most obvious in connection with the worship of the god *Soma*. The Soma juice has miraculous qualities, conferring might upon both gods and men. Indra is exhorted to drink the Soma juice in order to increase his might, and in I, 56-1 we have the line—"The Soma juice, which strengthens for great deeds."

The effect of this is to encourage the idea that religious satisfaction can be obtained by emphasising the lower aspects of human nature, and especially by physical participation. From the first there was probably a certain negative and ascetic colouring in this idea, due to the purely empirical discovery that ecstatic and apparently religious conditions could be produced by fasting and mortification of the body. When, through contact with the complexities of life, the higher powers of human nature awaken, the negative idea still persists, with the result that religious satisfaction appears to be obtainable only by the sacrifice of these higher powers. The world-reality is still materialistically conceived and is represented as an alien force, correspondence with which can be obtained only by the negation of the essential characteristic of humanity. It is a support of the lower elements only, and involves the denial of what man is coming dimly to regard as the most valuable parts of his own nature. Here we have the germ of the negative ascetic idea which pervades the whole of Indian philosophy.

When once this negative idea has crept in, it seems impossible to eradicate it. It spreads over the whole of experience. If the reality of the universe is alien to our higher experience, it may soon come to be regarded as alien to our experience altogether. With the advance of thought the ultimate reality may, indeed, cease to be regarded as material, but the influence of the original magical conceptions still remain, and we are no nearer a reconciliation of the human spirit with the divine. It has ceased to be material, but because it has been conceived from the point of view of purely intellectual, as distinct from ethical, speculation, it has become abstract. Thus the religious longing which still goes out towards it can be satisfied only by deliverance from the conditions of human life, and not by elevation and completion of these conditions.

We have thus travelled far from the primitive joyousness of much of the *Rig-Veda*, but at the same time have simply drawn out the logical consequences of many of the thoughts which are implicit in it. These thoughts obtain more explicit expression perhaps in the *Atharva-Veda*. Both from it and the *Rig-Veda* we may obtain numerous indications that we are within sight of the later developed conceptions of *Samsara* and *Karma* and *Mukti*, with their underlying idea that the world of human existence is a ceaseless meaningless round, a "bondage of everlasting sorrow," from which we may escape, but over which we cannot hope to obtain the victory. It is this longing for deliverance, rather than salvation, in the full sense of the term, which the philosophical thought of the *Upanishads* sets itself to satisfy, but we shall be content in this chapter with indicating the conditions out of which the longing arose, and the character of the solution which was being foreshadowed. Before philosophical thought proper began, the problem of life had become serious, if not distinctly gloomy, as regards the character of its setting.

Before closing this chapter we may refer to one or two other causes which deepened the sense of need for deliverance. Amongst these is the doctrine of transmigration, which seems to have crept into Indian thought between the Vedic period and the period of the *Upanishads*. In the *Rig-Veda* there are only vague hints of such a doctrine. There is evidence of a belief in immortality, coupled with more or less detailed imaginations of the lot of the soul in the other world.[1] In the *Atharva Veda* and the Brahmanas the details of the future life become fuller and the germs of a doctrine of transmigration appear. There is, further, a growing fear of falling into the power of death, and this is a point of the utmost importance. The emphasis is coming to be laid not so much upon a series of lives in another world, but upon a series of deaths, in which transformation we may see the effects of the tendency to negation which we have already noticed. There is thus preparation for the attitude of aversion.

It was comparatively easy to transfer the location of the series of future lives from another world to this, especially under the influence of beliefs prevalent amongst all primitive peoples. The common theory is that Indian thought borrowed this idea from alien

---

[1] Cf. *Rig-Veda* X, 16 and 58.

sources, but it is not likely that the Aryans received it in any very developed form, and the elaboration of the theory of a chain of existences was left to the philosophers of the incoming race and connected by them with the idea of retribution. Neither Max Müller nor Deussen will admit this borrowing, and regard the doctrine as a perfectly natural development within Indian thought itself. Still, there do seem to be traces of syncretism, and even in the *Upanishads* themselves there is a double set of ideas, which would seem to indicate a double source. The idea of borrowing also would explain the antithesis between the conception of transmigration and the negative mystical pantheism which we have seen to be characteristic of the earliest beginnings of Indian philosophical thought.

In this antithesis also we may find the explanation of the depressing influence which the doctrine of transmigration tended to exert. It might be thought that, as providing an escape from death, it would be essentially productive of happiness. But under the influence of the negative idea, aversion to death is transformed into aversion to life. If this life and its experiences are regarded as undesirable, a succession of lives would simply multiply the misery, for escape is not so easy a matter when an almost infinite succession of lives has to be reckoned with. Thus, though the doctrine may have been originally introduced for the purposes of consolation and reward, the rewards are lost sight of and attention is concentrated on the darker aspects. The future borrows its character from the sorrows of the present rather than its joys. The doctrine of transmigration, when combined with the doctrine of emancipation, becomes therefore a directly pessimistic influence, and greatly strengthens the desire for emancipation. Annihilation at the end of one life becomes a comfortable thought, when compared with the prospect which was now opening up. Men are denied even the sorry comfort of the thought of a speedy end of misery.

Of course, besides these religious and semi-religious tendencies, other influences were at work to increase the general sense of the gravity of the problems which were pressing for philosophical solution. But these hardly call for special mention, being amongst the most general conditions of life in any country. We may notice, however, that in India the contrast between wealth and poverty, and between despotism and helplessness, has in past times been more marked than in other lands. The population was divided into despots and those who were in subjection to them, and the division between wealth and poverty corresponded pretty closely to the political division. Such contrasts were certainly not so clearly marked in Vedic times, but they may have been beginning to make themselves felt by the time that philosophical speculation emerges. It may not be out of place also to mention the enervating influence of the climate, diminishing the zest of life, disposing men to seek for deliverance rather than development, and inducing patient acquiescence rather than persistent struggle.

CHAPTER II

The General Character of the Solution

WE have seen that by the time philosophical speculation begins the horizon of thought has become somewhat overcast and the outlook decidedly pessimistic. Some possible causes of this pessimism have been suggested, and further enquiry will show that these suggested causes continue their working into the philosophical period. They change their character, however, and what were at first only implicit tendencies become elevated to the rank of philosophical principles, which are applied in order to furnish a solution of the very problems which in their implicit form they had done so much to render acute. In other words, the solution of the problem may be found to consist simply in a carrying further of the very ideas which had made apparent the necessity of a solution. Perhaps, like the angel's spear, these ideas may be capable of curing the wounds which they themselves have caused? The answer to this question will become apparent as we proceed.

We have traced a growing consciousness of the need for deliverance, and the *Upanishads* set themselves definitely to meet this need. There is a dark background to all their thoughts. Men have felt themselves overwhelmed by the idea of the incomprehensible divine Unity, and the chief subject of speculation is the baffling characteristics of the world, both intellectual and moral. From the confusing diversity of human experience, having unity only in its painfulness, from the unending succession of lives presenting no prospect of improvement throughout the series, where was deliverance to be found?

This yearning after deliverance finds repeated expression. In the *Katha* Upanishad II, 6-7, we read—

"The wise man ceases to *grieve* when he knows the distinction of the Self from the senses"; and the Self which is the object of our striving is "free from old age, from death, or *grief*." It is the homeland of the soul which is sought for, and a man reaches it only after many wanderings, in the course of which he suffers many things. The world of finite experience from which we are to flee is one of misery, and in the contemplation of it there is nothing but pain. The reason of this pessimistic attitude is hinted at over and over again. It is the restricted and fleeting character of human experience. In the *Chhandogya* Upanishad we may trace the same ideas. Cf. VII, 23-1. "There is no bliss in anything finite"; and again, VII, 26-1, "He who sees this [the Self] does not see death, nor illness nor pain." Here also we find that it is the injustice and inequalities of the earthly lot which prompt to questions. "If the body is blind or lame or poverty-stricken, what will be the lot of the Self?" asks Indra in the same Upanishad.

The perplexed, pathetic tone is evident throughout. A recent writer, Mr. P. L. Sen, draws attention to this and emphasises the negative standpoint of the Upanishads. "The sources of pain in life are innumerable. So far as we can see, the quantity of misery far outbalances that of enjoyment, and as to what lies beyond, the mysterious character is not at all likely to turn the scale." Cf. *Philosophy of the Vedanta*, Bk. I, 4.

It may be pointed out, however, that nothing is gained by drawing attention to this pessimistic background of the Upanishads, seeing that dissatisfaction with the existing state of things is the pre-condition of all philosophical investigation. This may be readily admitted, but at the same time it may be urged that this dissatisfaction varies considerably in degree, and where it is excessive it is well to draw attention to it and to the degree of its pressure, because in such cases of excess we may see most clearly the influence which the conditions of origin exercise upon the character of the solution. Now, it can be shown that any considerable pressure of pessimistic ideas does exercise a weakening influence, both practically and theoretically. Chesterton, in his recent book on Dickens, points out that a pessimist is never so good a reformer as an optimist, and the "man who believes life to be excellent is the man who alters it most." Where pessimism is to any extent prevalent as a mental attitude, conservatism is the resulting practical attitude, and a consideration of Indian social conditions will easily illustrate the truth of this remark. In the theoretical sphere, also, the unfortunate influence of an excessively gloomy preliminary conception of the problems to be solved is not easily shaken off. It has impressed itself very deeply upon the mind of the philosopher, and he is inclined to come far too quickly to the conclusion that the world of experience lies in hopeless confusion. His pessimism is at the outset so strong that he hardly dares hope for victory, he can only sigh for deliverance. This despair often goes a long way towards determining the character of his speculative philosophy and the solutions which it obtains. The preliminary pessimism of the Indian philosopher is often so strong as to make him almost take for granted the insolubility of his problems, or find a solution in what is virtually little more than a confession of insolubility.

Further, if the human mind is obsessed by a feeling of hopelessness, it is left with insufficient room for free and independent speculation. The weight of the burden is so great that one must hasten to get rid of it, and a demand for a rapid solution of problems becomes insistent. Perhaps here we may find one reason for the mixture—or even confusion—of purely speculative with religious and ethical motive, which is constantly found in Indian philosophy. Of course one is far from demurring, especially in India, to any practical application of philosophy, and, if we possess a faith in the unity of human experience, we must admit that the philosophical and religious motives must ultimately coincide. But the point to be insisted on here is that, if practical and emotional needs are too urgent, there is often a temptation to hasten unduly the solution of speculative problems. It often happens that instead of being solved the difficulties of the problem are concealed in a mystical haze. The mind which is consumed with the desire for deliverance, and is not unfamiliar with the claims of mystical intuition, becomes unduly receptive, and arguments, which are admittedly not cogent from an intellectual standpoint, are accepted under the influence of religious motives and practical needs. An indication of such a danger may be found in the prevalence of the idea of two orders of knowledge, so different from one another that sometimes what is true in one sphere may be untrue in another. This fondness for the distinction between the esoteric and the exoteric, combined with an exceedingly facile transition from the one to the other, is both dangerous in itself and disastrous to the completeness of a philosophy. It is, however, a very present help in time of trouble.

From what has been said we may see the propriety of making special reference to the pessimistic background of Indian philosophy. We have here more than the "divine discontent" from which all philosophy admittedly springs. There is rather a sense of weariness and discouragement, the influence of which never entirely disappears. It is not altogether untrue to describe Indian philosophy as "springing from lassitude and a desire for eternal rest."[1]

We should, however, be passing an unjust judgment if, in proceeding to a more positive characterisation of the general solution offered, we were to allow these considerations to weigh unduly. Though the intense desire for relief was dominant, and was, as just indicated, somewhat prejudicial to genuine philosophical search, we must not think that it was so dominant as to exclude speculative construction or stifle the desire for it. The world with which the thinkers of the period had to deal, presented itself not merely as something to be escaped from, but also as

---

[1] Chailley, *Administrative Problems*, p. 67.

something to be explained. It was not complete in itself. The phenomenal many provoked an enquiry into the one spirit, which moved through the things of nature and was manifest also in the life-breath of the seekers after truth. What was it, and what was its relation to them and to their world? Sometimes they seemed almost to grasp it, as, in an intensity of devotion, they recited their sacred hymns. The thrill of enthusiasm was the movement in them of the divine, and they were possessed of a strange, mystic harmony, binding themselves and God and the universe into one.

Surely they could penetrate into this mystery a little way, and, in the desire to do so, their philosophy arose. We have here a continuation of the spirit which underlies all attempts at explanatory mythology, and of which we have already received hints in the Vedas. It is the desire to get to the regions beyond sense-experience, to "where the other side of the sun is seen."[1] The conception of the giant Purusha[2] and his literal dismemberment is now transformed into the conception of a primal principle evolving into natural phenomena. The speculative note which was struck in the Vedas becomes much more dominant in the Upanishads.

The very word "Upanishad" seems to signify speculative intensity. The most generally accepted meaning is that of "session," the sitting round a teacher in order to receive instruction. From the idea of instruction received by sitting very near a teacher we pass to the idea of "secret doctrine." Sometimes also the term is interpreted as meaning "destruction or approach." The underlying idea in all usages is that of a doctrine, which, received from a teacher, provides a way of approach to God and destroys all error. The negative state from which deliverance is sought is also conceived of somewhat intellectually. It is not merely a state of misery but also a state of error, and conversely, what is desired is truth which can be speculatively established. The character of the solution which

[1] Rig-Veda IX, 113, 10. [2] Cf. X, 90.

is sought for presupposes a very considerable degree of intellectual development, and intellectual interests are never lost sight of, though we might not be able to go so far as to agree with Barth that the Upanishads are "much more instinct with the spirit of speculative daring than the sense of suffering and weariness."[1]

Further, the circumstances in which the Upanishads were composed were favourable to pure speculation. The inquiries they record belong explicitly to a period of life when practical interests were no longer supreme, when the active duties of life had been exchanged for a period of quiet contemplation in the forest, when those who were both learned and aged might gather round some teacher for undistracted study of the ultimate mysteries. Moreover, the free creative spirit, which is necessary for all constructive philosophy, was decidedly in the ascendant. Although the influence of the Vedas was strong, their authority was not so oppressive as to bind intellectual activity entirely to a minute consideration of the exact language of ancient philosophical precepts or a ceaseless recapitulation of traditional ideas. While perhaps the complete sense of freedom from authority expressed in *Gita* II, 42, to the effect that "As great as is the use of a well which is surrounded on all sides by overflowing water, so great and no greater is the use of the Vedas to a Brahman endowed with true knowledge" had not yet been reached; yet there was, especially in the older *Upanishads*, a realisation of liberty sufficient to support a genuine search after truth.

This sense of mystery and the desire to penetrate it is manifest at the very beginning of the *Katha Upanishad*. Naciketas, having been offered and having refused several boons of a more or less material character, such as long life and wealth, and also some relating to the heavenly life, says, "No, that on which there is this doubt, O Death, tell us what there is in that great hereafter. Naciketas does not choose another boon, but that which enters into the hidden world."[2] An

[1] *Religions of India*, p. 84. [2] *Katha Upanishad* I, 1-29.

ever-recurring refrain in the first few sections of the *Brihadaranyaka* (probably amongst the oldest sections of the Upanishads) is, "Lead me from darkness unto light, from the unreal to the real." In the *Chhandogya Upanishad* (VI, 3), the question is asked, "Hast thou sought for the instruction by which also the Unheard becomes heard, the Unintelligible intelligible, and the Unknown known?" and in the same Upanishad the typical teacher is said to have shown to his pupil, "after all his faults had been rubbed out, the bank on the other side of darkness."[1] When with this genuine speculative interest there is combined the more practical desire for release from the confusions, miseries, and disappointments of the actual world, we have a complex motive of sufficient intensity to carry us far into the region of the hitherto unknown.

The solution which is offered is mainly of a negative and mystical character, consisting in the transformation of our ordinary attitude to the world. The data of our ordinary consciousness are to be rejected as illusory, and their particularity is to be denied. We are to retire within ourselves, and in finding our true selves we are also to find God—a unity in which all differences are merged. We are not summoned to make any change upon our world, but rather to turn away from it altogether, with an upward movement which will not cease until the absolute unity is reached, the Reality over against which all else is unreal.

The aim of religious and philosophical thought which is here set forth is a high and noble one, and though in order that men may reach their goal many crude devices are suggested and many survivals of primitive thought and custom are made use of, yet the goal itself is always kept in view and there is a seriousness in the whole endeavour. For the purposes of exposition we may describe the endeavour under two aspects—(1) the denial of the particularity of the world of our ordinary experience; (2) the effort to identify the human spirit with the divine so as to reach absolute

[1] Chhandogya VII, 26, 2.

unity. We must always remember that these aspects can be treated separately only for the purposes of exposition, and that in the Indian philosophical consciousness they are intimately bound up with each other.

(1) The first step then is to distrust the empirical data of the senses. They introduce us to the realm of particularity, of objects in space and in time, distracting our interests and exciting individualistic desires. Salvation can be attained only by transcending such a world as this. We must shake off every mode of personal existence and reach the "fontal unity of undifferenced being." All the details of our world of ordinary experience must be crushed together into a unity, and, if they will not go into the narrow mould which has been provided for them, they must be negated. No matter what differences of value we may have been accustomed to ascribe to the various parts of our ordinary world, it must all be given up, both the things of higher and the things of lower importance. Whether we are viewing the things of the world from a scientific or a practical point of view, whether they are objects of perception or objects of desire, it makes no difference, the sentence of philosophical annihilation must be passed upon them all. Thought may think a plurality of objects, but thought itself is one and it must return to its own nature, having gained the victory; and plurality must disappear.[1] "As unreal forms of being and as one will he be thought, but he who thinks is always one, therefore, unity retains the victory."

Another way of putting the matter is to say that all the content of the ordinary world is made up of names, which names supply a basis of individuality for particular things, and encourage us in an attribution of a reality to them to which they have no sufficient right. This point of view anticipates to some extent that of the mediæval nominalists, only that for the nominalist the names served the purpose of giving a fictitious reality to general notions, whereas here they perform this service for particular things.

[1] Cf. *Mandukya Upanishad* II, 13.

This inversion of ordinary experience and contempt for the immediate suggest a parallel with the procedure of Descartes, who also resolutely rejected all received knowledge and halted not until he had reached his fundamental formula of "*Cogito ergo sum*." There is, however, an important difference which should be noted. The motive of Descartes was to find a secure basis for science and philosophy, a point from which he could return to the world of experience and construct a trustworthy system of knowledge in regard to it. In the Upanishads, however, we have not this positive return. We are compelled for the most part to be content with the negative movement, and our philosophical guides, having reduced all things to a unity, care little for any methods by which this unity may be shown to realise itself in difference. There is, at least, no return in a purely logical manner, however much, by means of mythological makeshifts and in concession to popular ideas, the contrast between their speculative position and their practical experience may afterwards be softened.

This suggests a question as to the exact nature of the distinction which they drew between phenomenon and noumenon. It is certainly obvious that no reality was attributed to phenomena in their separate particularity. But the question still remains, whether the phenomena retained any vestige of reality when their intrinsic connection with the ultimate unity was perceived, or whether an uncompromising judgment of illusion should be pronounced upon them. This introduces the subject of *Maya*, and would involve a presentation of the controversy between Sankara and Ramanuja. Into this controversy the limits of space forbid us to enter. It may be sufficent to say here, that the tendency is mainly, though not exclusively, in the direction of absolute negation. Some of the metaphors and illustrations used seem, indeed, when fully analysed, to allow a subsidiary reality to phenomena. When it is said, *e.g.*, that from one piece of clay all things may be known, this does not imply that the reality of the clay is destroyed when it is distributed amongst particular things. Similarly, the metaphor of rivers flowing into the sea and losing their name and form is an exceedingly common one, but does not necessarily imply the destruction of the reality of the water which originally composed the separate rivers. Still we cannot bind the teachers of the Upanishads to a full analysis of their metaphors, and it must, on the whole, be admitted, that the purpose for which the metaphors are introduced is to exhibit the unreality of all plurality. We may discover subsequently, however, that it is impossible fully to carry out this purpose, but still the world which is denied is mainly regarded as illusory. Indeed, this is the logical outcome of denying all value to it.

The existence of the world which is denied is not due to any actual causative principle, but to ignorance, *i.e.*, to something which has within it from the outset the germs of negation. Perhaps it is in the later Upanishads that we find the conception of illusion most explictly stated, *e.g.*, in the *Svetasvatara Upanishads XX*, *I*, *10* we read, "The one God regulates nature and the self. By meditating on Him the world-illusion is completely removed." The *Mandukya Upanishad* (belonging to the Atharva Veda) III, 48, tells us that "this is the highest saving knowledge, that there is no becoming." Many authorities hold the opinion that the doctrine of *Maya* is nothing but a late introduction. Colebrooke, *e.g.*, says, "The notion that the versatile world is an entire illusion and that all that passes to the apprehension of the waking individual is but a phantasy does not appear to be the doctrine of the text of the Vedanta." Colebrooke's opinion is followed by Jacobs and Dr. Barnett; and Pundit S. N. Tattvabhushan refuses to believe that even the *Svetasvatara* explicitly teaches this doctrine. On the other hand, Professor Dutt Shastri holds the opinion that such thinkers are entirely mistaken, and that "though the word is found for the first time in the *Svetasvatara*, the idea may be traced to the later stage of the Vedic civilisation," and, though not in a systematic and organic form, is already found in the *Rig-Veda* and the Upanishads."[1]

[1] *The Doctrine of Maya*, p. 36.

Perhaps the truth may be that the Upanishads are, in this matter, striving towards a position which they never quite reached. A middle position, which would compel us neither to an entire negation of the world nor to any particularising assertion of its reality. As Dr. Thibaut says, "The great error which the *Upanishads* admonish us to relinquish is, that things have a separate individual existence and are not bound together by the bonds of all of them being effects of Brahman or Brahma himself."[1] They are aiming at an ideal of totality rather than of negation, and only the particular which is viewed out of connection with this totality is to be regarded as altogether illusion. The teaching of the metaphor of clay, *e.g.*, would be, that if we were to assert that the various pots, etc., are not made of clay or have no connection with clay, we should be under an illusion. From this, however, it does not follow that when their nature as clay has been fully recognised they have then to be regarded as unreal. Similarly, if finite things are viewed as detached from the whole, they are unreal, but if their connection with the whole is understood, their reality may still be asserted.

Nevertheless, as has been already hinted, this was an ideal of unified knowledge which the Upanishads never fully reached, and it is doubtful whether we can consider it to be their ultimate position. Of course we cannot impulsively say that a philosophy does not hold a position just because it has not fully established it, but the case is different when the philosophy has turned away from this position, when, because of the difficulties of occupying the position, it has virtually said that the position need not be occupied at all. Yet this is the direction of the main tendency in the teaching of the Upanishads. The writers find insuperable difficulties in connecting their unity with their diversity, and instead of saying that this connection must still be kept in view as the goal of knowledge they have recourse to the expedient of denying the finite world altogether, and all its difficulties along with it. Thus they reach the position

[1] Sankara's Commentary, p. 114.

of abstract idealism, which seems to be dominant in many parts of the Upanishads. It may have been only as the controversy went on that the difficulties of a naïvely pantheistic point of view became apparent, but the Maya doctrine seems to have become almost indispensable when the difficulties were realised and the manifoldness of the world had to be reconciled with the unity of the first principle. The plurality could not be deduced from the unity, and so the unity was denied altogether.

In order, however, that we may be in a position to deny anything, we must be able to form some sort of conception of it, and even this temporary conception requires an explanation. The only explanation which can consistently be admitted by a negative philosophy is one which carries with it at the outset the suggestion of the illusory character of that which is to be explained. Such an explanation we find in the use of the principle of Avidya (Ignorance). This principle involves not only what we might call empirical ignorance, but empirical knowledge as well, *i.e.*, not only the negative idea usually associated with the word ignorance, but the positive idea of false knowledge. It includes all knowledge which presupposes the reality of the objects of ordinary experience, all knowledge which takes account of plurality.

It is of more importance for our present purpose to note the metaphysical character of this ignorance. It is not merely subjective ignorance, but world-ignorance. We may understand the transition from the usual point of view if we remember that this Avidya includes not only empirical ignorance, but empirical knowledge. We may thus easily pass from the negative conception of ignorance, which confines us to this knowledge, to the knowledge itself, which is included in this ignorance. But this body of empirical knowledge itself demands an explanation, and the explanation which is supplied is that the power which is responsible for our limitations is also responsible for what is known under these limitations, *i.e.*, the explanation in both cases is ignorance. Or we may state the process in a slightly different way.

Ignorance is conceived of not only as particular ignorance but as universal ignorance, *i.e.*, it is ignorance which attaches to God as well as to man. It is described in *Svetasvatara* I, 3, as "the own power of God concealed by its emanations." But with the ultimate reality we cannot distinguish between thought and existence. Therefore, misleading thought is also misleading power of bringing into existence.

Ignorance, then, has this twofold power of obstructing our view of the real nature of things, and of giving an apparent reality to what is ultimately unknown. The very selection of the term is an admission of mystery, and at the same time a putting forward of an excuse that it is unnecessary to attempt to penetrate the mystery. Ignorance is something which, in its own nature, cannot be understood. That which is unintelligent in the subjective use becomes the unintelligible in the objective or metaphysical use. As has been said, "He who would know Avidya is like a man who should rush to see darkness by means of a far-shining torch." We are further mentally prepared for accepting, to the greatest possible extent, the illusory character of the world, if we find not only that we are mistaken in thinking that there is a world of finite objects, but that this world is based on a principle which is itself illusion incarnate.

If we are disposed to accuse the Upanishad teachers of explaining a positive by a negative, we must not embarrass their position unduly by taking too positive and crass a view of matter. We must remember, that according to their theory it is not a positive which is explained by a negative, but a negative by a negative, the unreal by the unreal. The illustration of a conjurer may help us to understand the position. In watching the tricks of a conjurer, we, if we think the results are real, are labouring under a mistake, but to this mistake of ours corresponds the power of the conjurer to produce what we imagine we have seen, which power he does not really possess but which we attribute to him. Similarly, to the world of illusion corresponds the illusory power of

God, which power is relative only to our ignorance. This illustration, however, covers over more difficulties than it solves. We feel inclined to point out that the conjurer does, after all, produce an actual result: it is only our interpretation of it which is mistaken. Further, his power is a real power of producing, and its reality is unaffected by our mistaken interpretation of the product. Even an illusion must have a cause, and the illusion of a finite world is not exempt from this law. From nothing, nothing can come—not even an illusion. We may mistake the rope for a snake, but the rope must, after all, be there as at least the fact of a rope before we can mistake it for a snake.

Thus we find that the explanation of the ordinary world as the product of Ignorance is not free from difficulties. We may, however, concentrate upon the idea that denial of the world by removal of this Nescience is possible, and we may consider some of the stages through which we pass towards its removal. If we are thinking of external conditions we have the doctrine of the four stages or *Asramas*. The stage of the *Brahmacharin*, when the Vedas are studied under the guidance of a teacher; the stage of the *Grihastha* or householder, during which the ordinary duties of society are undertaken and sacrifices are peformed; the stage of the *Vanaprastha*, when the devotee betakes himself to the wood to spend his time in fasting and in penance; and finally, the stage of the *Sannyasi*, who has no fixed place of abode, who is without possessions, who has overcome desire for individual existence, and longs only for release from the world and absorption into the universal.

If we consider the matter more subjectively as a process in the individual soul, we find that it is also through various stages of consciousness that we rise upwards to the supreme position. The guiding passage for the exposition of this doctrine is *Chhandogya* VIII, 7 to 12, where the conversation between Indra and Prajapati is recorded, and where Indra is represented as led on from one stage to another by gradual instruction. To each subjective stage there corresponds a certain mode of conceiving the universe which is ever becoming more adequate. At the first, or walking stage, both body and mind are active; at the next stage, or dreaming stage, only the mind is active, but the conditions of individuality are still operative. The self may live in a world of his own creation, but the distinctions between the Self and otherselves, and between the self and objects, still remains. So we must rise to the third, or last, stage of dreamless sleep, at which we reach absorption in the Prajna Atma, or true self—the universal subject of thought. The self is conscious of being the Universe, and all distinctions are merged in an absolute identity.[1] "This, indeed, is his true form in which his wishes are fulfilled, in which the Self only is his wish, in which no wish is left—free from any sorrow. Then a father is not a father, a mother is not a mother, the worlds not worlds, the gods not gods, the Vedas not Vedas." All differences are negated.

Sometimes, especially in the later Upanishads, it is maintained that there is still another stage. The state of dreamless sleep is felt to be inadequate, for the reasons that it is liable to be interrupted, and that it is purely negative—"the dreamer knows wrongly, the sleeper knows nothing at all. Both are wrong."[2] A state of being is desired which shall be "coincident with absolute wakefulness" and approach to the self-luminousness of Brahman, and in which also there will be absolute union with the universal subject. Such a highest state (*turiya* or *chaturtha*) is of course indescribable with the indescribableness of Brahma himself. We must be content with the spiritual consummation of identity, and must not attempt to put it into words.

A somewhat more elaborate description of the soul's progress in denial of the world is given in the doctrine of the five sheaths (kosa). It does not differ in any essential point from the process we have just been considering. Only the metaphors are changed, and they

---

[1] Cf. *Brihadaranyaka* IV, 3-21. [2] *Mandukya* II, 15.

are more analytical. There is the same mingling of psychological and cosmical conception. The first four sheaths are regarded as shells or husks, which have to be stripped off, in order that we may perceive the true self in the fifth phase, with which alone we can be content. The first sheath (*annamaya*) is the sheath of food; and, when covered by this, we identify the self with the body. Next comes the *pranamaya* sheath, or sheath of breath, in connection with which the self is still identified with the body, but with the body in its dynamical rather than its statical aspect. We have gone beyond matter and reached a conception very much akin to the force of the modern physicist. With the third stage, or *manamaya* sheath, we enter the mental region. The mind is conceived of as passive and psychologically on the sensitive level, dependent on external impression. Religiously it is dependent on authority. With the *vijnanamaya kosa* we reach the conception of the understanding subject, the reason which gives unity to all our experiences; but, as this stage still involves the duality of subject and object, it must be transcended by a position in which there is absolute identity, in which subject and object are one. Such a position is reached in the *anandamaya kosa*, the sheath of bliss, involving the entire destruction of individuality and the consummation of absorption.

But, however we may describe the process of the soul's ascent, we find that each onward step is a step of further negation, until we reach the universal self, "into which all things pass away, as the ocean is the one thing into which all rivers flow." We are called upon to enter upon a process of relentless abstraction from the so-called reality of everything finite, and from all our intellectual and practical interests in finite things. All difference is simply a matter of names and of illusions. We must strip off, one by one, the coverings with which our senses have invested particular things, and we shall find that while these coverings have seemed to cover reality, it is, properly speaking, nothingness which they conceal. We shall, therefore, not be hindered by them in our search for the pure undifferenced unity. "We shall become lords of the world of time, by turning our backs upon it." Max Müller, in his *Lectures on the Vedanta*, p. 137, describes the extremes to which the process is carried, "The process of negation, or what may to be called abstraction, goes on till every leaf of the flower is plucked off, and nothing remains but the calyx, or the seed, the inconceivable Brahman, the Self of the world."

(2) We have already touched frequently upon the second part of the subject, which is here under consideration, *viz.*, the effort to realise the oneness of the individual soul with the universal soul, the Atman with Brahman. In discovering our fundamental nature, or self, we discover the ultimate being of the universe. To find out this identity is the object of all our searching, and it is from failure to reach it that all our troubles, both theoretical and practical, arise. Brahman is all that is, and yet we attribute reality to the objects of perception and value the limited impulses of our souls. We are like a bird tied with a rope. We are continually trying to escape from the rope, whereas we should find peace for our souls if we would only return in quietness to the centre where the string is attached.[1]

The fundamental teaching of the Upanishads is perhaps contained in these two verses. In one half verse, "I shall tell you what has been taught in thousands of volumes: Brahman is true and the world is false, the soul is Brahman and nothing else"; and again, "There is nothing worth gaining, there is nothing worth enjoying but Brahman alone, for he who knows Brahman is Brahman." Pundit S. N. Tattvabhushan thus describes the aim of Upanishad thought, "To think and feel and act as if—as is really the case—I were the universe: this is the grand ideal which the Upanishads and the *Gita* set up before their followers, an ideal which guides the practical conduct and devotional exercises of all true Hindu theists."

---

[1] Cf. *Chhandogya* VI, 8-2.

The fundamental formula is "*tat tvam asi*," which may be taken as indicating the equation of the individual self with the universe, and of the universe with the Self in the highest sense, the result being a pure undifferenced unity beyond which there is nothing, and which itself can be described ultimately only by negative predicates. The doctrine in which such teaching is conveyed is called *advaita-vada*, the doctrine of non-duality, described by Prof. Macdonell as an idealistic monism. All is One, and the One is Myself. One of the texts which gives the greatest amount of support to the doctrine of identity is *Chhandogya* III, 14, 4: "He, from whom all works, all desires, all sweet odours and tastes proceed, who embraces all this, who never speaks, who is never surprised, he, myself within the heart, is that Brahman."

The identification which is ultimately hoped for is considered possible only by an extreme spiritualising of the individual Self and the Universal Self. The goal is no absorption of ourselves in the dead matter of an unspiritual universe. The ultimate principle is looked upon as spiritual. The name *Brahman*, according to some interpretations, originally meant prayer. Then, by emphasis upon the idea that human prayer is more potent than the gods, the word came to be used for the eternal principle itself. It would be a mistake to build too much upon such an etymology, but it may serve to indicate the presence of a vague idea of correspondence between ultimate Being and the desires of man.

The two terms, Brahman and Atman, are to be regarded as complementary and reciprocally interpretative. The relation between them, as conceived by Sankara, is, that "Brahman denotes the term to be defined (viseshyam) and Atman that which defines it (viseshanan), that by Brahman the limitation implied in Atman is removed, and by Atman the conception of Brahman as a divinity to be worshipped is condemned"[1] It might also be described by saying that the Atman is the

[1] Cf. Deussen, *Upanishads*, p. 86.

ultimate attainment of philosophical speculation, but when that which is thus attained is constrained to cosmological service, it is called Brahman, the caution being always observed that Brahman is never to be viewed as out of connection with Atman, never even to be associated so externally with Atman as to make the relation between them that of worshipped and worshipper.

Any adequate characterisation of the ultimate unity is impossible. Sankara warns us against regarding the ordinary world as real by attributing subjective qualities to the object, but he would hold it equally disastrous to attribute objective qualities to the subject. In other words, we must not imagine that the self can ever be made an object and considered as other objects. This warning is a continuation of the teaching of the *Brihadaranyaka Upanishad* III, 4, 2, "Thou could'st not see the true seer of sight, thou could'st not hear the true hearer of hearing, nor perceive the perceiver of perception, nor know the knower of knowledge. This is thy Self who is within all." Again, in III, 8, 11: "That Brahman sees, but is unseen; he hears, but is unheard; he perceives, but is unperceived."

The truth is that Brahman, who is also the Atman, is too near us for characterisation. We cannot stand apart from him, and view him and describe him as other objects are viewed and described. In a sense, we are blinded by excess of light: "We are like men who turn from the reflection of light in other things to the sun, and who, though they are looking at pure light, are so dazzled by it that they can see nothing at all. So, in turning our souls to the unity, which is the presupposition of our consciousness of other things, we lose sight of every image of sense or imagination, and we are even carried beyond all definite thought by which we can distinguish one object from another. We are, so to speak, in perfect light where we can distinguish as little as in perfect darkness."[1]

---

[1] Caird, *Evolution of Theology in the Greek Philosophers*.

If we attempt to impose any predicates upon the ultimate Being, we must remember that they do not really apply. They are like the alloy which the goldsmith mixes with the pure gold in order that he may work it, but which afterwards must be extracted even by fire. The very confusion and contradictoriness of our ordinary predicates ought to open our eyes to their inadequacy. The Upanishads, by exhibiting this contradictoriness, take one of the most effective methods of emphasising their fundamental teaching. Over and over again, pairs of opposite predicates are applied evidently with the view that they may cancel each other, and so set us free for the employment of higher categories, or drive us beyond the use of categories altogether. Spatial contrasts are the most popular, but many others are also brought into service; and so the confusion goes on, illustrating the impossible attempt to characterise the characterless. We are forced to the conclusion that our ordinary predicates are useless, and that before Brahman words and thinking fail. Max Müller puts the matter rightly when he says, "Of the Self beyond the veil we can know nothing, beyond that it is—and this, too, in a way different from all other knowledge."[1]

Nevertheless, there are traces of positive characterisation, and these may be summed up in the formula, "sat-cit-ananda," which appears in the later Upanishads. It may be profitable to examine this formula for a little before we bring this chapter to an end. Is it an adequate defence against the charge of empty abstraction?

In choosing the predicate of Being, and using the neuter form of the word Brahma, one might be supposed to be committed to the least possible amount of assertion. The neuter is neither male nor female. It seems to imply a vague expansive power, higher than either masculine or feminine, capable of becoming everything, but as yet nothing, the centre of primitive life from which all things issue forth. For the very reason that this predicate gives us so little of positive character,

[1] *Lectures on the Vedanta*, p. 69.

we expect that it will at least be trustworthy, and that, when we have said that a thing is simply Being and nothing more, we shall be allowed to rest in this position. But we are hurried on. As soon as we have said that Brahman is being, we find that we may equally well use the predicate "not-Being," or, at least, the Upanishads would leave us entirely uncertain as to which predicate we ought to decide upon. In the *Chhandogya Upanishad* VI, 2, 2, we read, "Only that which *is*, was in the beginning, one only without a second." In the *Taittiriya* II, 7, we get exactly the opposite statement, "In the beginning non-Being, indeed, was this."

These contradictories imply rather inadequacy than confusion of thought. The opposite predicates, Being and non-Being, are an attempt to express the inexpressible. It is no new difficulty with which they are attempting to deal. We find traces of it in the *Rig-Veda* X, 129, 1. "In the beginning there was neither being nor non-being," and the contradiction here indicated pervades the whole of subsequent Indian thought. The underlying feeling seems to be that as soon as we have used the predicate Being, we must enter a double caution. We must not think for a moment that the ultimate Being is Being in the empirical sense. He is *not-Being* from the empirical point of view. He is the original and unmanifest, who has not yet assumed name and form, and, therefore, cannot be brought into the sphere of the empirical. At the same time, from the transcendental point of view he is positively Being: it would be a mistake to regard him as a negation.

Or we might put it another way, and say that the distinction between Being and non-Being is really an empirical one, and Brahman transcends this distinction. In the words of the *Mundaka Upanishad* II, 2-1, "He is higher than that which is and that which is not." He is above Being in the empirical sense, but at the same time he cannot be called Non-Being, for to speak thus would be still to occupy the empirical point of view, which in relation to Brahman is illegitimate. Hunt, in his *Essay on Pantheism*, p. 9, seems to have caught the spirit of the whole teaching. "He is not only called Being, but lest that word should fail to express his infinitude, he is also said to be non-being; not in the sense that matter is said not to exist, not because he is less than being, but because he is greater than all being. Our thoughts of existence are too mean to be applied to him."

Thus, out of the predicate of Being we get little except a confession of the inadequacy of our conceptions. Does the predicate of thought, *chit*, carry us further? This expresses, indeed, the belief that Brahman is not lower than thought, but at the same time the thought or knowledge which is ascribed to him is not any kind of thought with which we are familiar, and is the negation of all ordinary knowledge. Brahman certainly cannot be the subject of cognition, for this would mean that he is liable to modification, and to conceive him thus would be inconsistent with his absolute truth and infinity. It would, at least, imply the duality of subject and object. In the *Mandukya Upanishad* V, 7, it is said that Brahman is "neither internally nor externally cognitive, neither conscious nor unconscious." Here, again, we have the twofold caution indicated above. In saying that Brahman is not conscious, we mean that we cannot ascribe to him the duality involved in ordinary thought; in saying that he is not unconscious, we mean that he is at least not lower than thought. The term "self-luminousness" has been used to describe this pure and abstract thought, but it is difficult to put any consciousness into this somewhat vague phrase.

The predicate, "bliss," is also almost entirely negative. It has been described as "bliss without the fruition of happiness." It is no active enjoyment or consciousness of the perfect and unimpeded exercise of capacity. It is rather the complete consciousness of deliverance from anything that is not-bliss, and especially from miseries attendant on connection with the empirical world. For the worshipper who would reach Brahman it is the state of dreamless sleep, the negation of anything we would describe as happiness in our ordinary experience. It is the subjective state which results after putting off the last sheath separating us from ultimate Being, and, as applied to the Ultimate Being himself, it connotes absolute self-absorption, the soporific sinking into reality, without disturbance from any particular thought or particular interest.

We seem, therefore, driven to the conclusion that the only way we can describe the ultimate reality is by means of negative predicates. The attitude which we finally take up is described in another oft-recurring formula in the Upanishads—"*neti, neti*" (it is not so, it is not so). This negation is not to be applied to Brahman himself. As the Vedanta Sutra has it, "The clause, 'Not so, not so,' denies of Brahma the suchness which forms the topic of discussion."[1] The Vedantist and the followers of Upanishad thought, generally, would vehemently protest against the accusation that his ultimate is wholly negative. He would assert that he has reached Entity and not Nonentity.

At the same time, he can hardly answer satisfactorily the challenge that he should either give more positive meaning to the predicates of his ultimate Being, or acquiesce in the charge of negation. It would seem, indeed, as if thought must of necessity overleap itself when it reaches the pitch of abstraction which has just been indicated. In attempting to reach an absolute reality which is set in opposition to all ordinary experience, we find that we have reached what is little better than nothing. As Mr. L. P. Jacks says, "In the whole realm of thought there is no partition so thin as that which divides God from nothing, and such is the eagerness of the soul in its flight godwards that it constantly breaks through and plunges into the abyss on the other side. When once philosophy has reached the point of conceiving God as the only True, the only Real, the moment has come for thought to return upon itself. Not a step further can be taken, and the warning to turn back is peremptory. If thought neglects this

---

[1] Cf. *Vedanta Sutras*, III, 2-22.

warning, and tries to refine once more its last refinement . . . . it passes the boundary line between God and nothing, and enters the realm from which there is no return."[1]

We are almost inclined to say that the thought of the Upanishads has neglected this warning. It has leapt from the knowable to the unknowable, and reached the realm of blank darkness and silence. The reality which it professes to reach is altogether unrelated to anything that we know by way of ordinary experience, and so we can hardly say whether it is reality or unreality, whether it is something or everything or nothing. The danger hinted at should be remembered, in view of the problem of the effect of such a philosophy on our sense of the value of life. Blank darkness is not cheerful, and reaction follows upon excessive straining of thought. There is need, sometimes, of the warning of Goethe, that "man is not born to solve the problem of the universe, but to find out where the problem begins and then to restrain himself within the limits of the comprehensible."[2]

---

[1] *Hibbert Journal*, Jan., 1908. [2] *Eckermann* I, p. 272.

CHAPTER III

The Pantheism and Pessimism of the System

IN the preceding chapter we have attempted to exhibit the strongly negative tendency of the main teaching of the Upanishads. One part of our task in this chapter will be to show that we are justified in describing the system of teaching, even in relation to this main tendency, as pantheistic. But before entering upon this somewhat controversial topic, we shall briefly refer to certain elements in the teaching which indicate a pantheism of a distinctly naturalistic type.

In treating of the world which was to be denied, and the conceptions of *Maya* and *Avidya* which aided that denial, we found that many difficulties had arisen in adjusting the abstract idealism involved in these conceptions to the requirements of ordinary experience. Empiricism is never far away from idealism, and the pendulum of thought swings from one to the other. If, under the influence of an abstract idealism, the value of the data of our ordinary experience has been denied, sooner or later these data claim their rights again and demand recognition. There is continued oscillation between the abstract point of view—which often claims somewhat unjustifiably to be the point of view of pure philosophy—and popular beliefs which have grown up, without much conscious reflection, out of traditional mythology, ritual, and general practice. Ordinary procedure cannot be permanently reversed. The Eleatics may assert the sole reality of Being, but they have also to reckon with the school of Heraclitus. Plato, following them, may attempt to confine his thought to the pure motionless world of Ideas, but in order to complete his philosophy he has to make some attempt to realise the connection between the Ideas and the world of ordinary phenomena.

So in the Upanishads also, the need is felt of assigning greater importance to the facts of ordinary experience. We may deny the reality of our world theoretically, but we have still to live in it practically, and therefore we must make some adjustment of our thought to it, even though the necessity for such adjustment may be only temporary.

The method of adaptation which we are now to examine was not necessarily subsequent in time to the complete establishment of the abstract position. Further, the adaptation must have been constantly renewed, as ever and again the necessity of adjustment to the world of ordinary experience made itself felt. Pantheism has always a double movement, like the systole and diastole of the heart. There is the movement away from the world of experience, and then, as inevitably, the movement back to experience again. We wish now to seize the movement of thought at that stage in the constantly repeated process where, having arrived at the abstract position, it turns back upon the way it has come, and seeks to adapt itself once more to the everyday experience which it is uncomfortably conscious of having left too far behind.

The motives to this movement of thought are various. As we have just seen, inversion of ordinary experience in itself produces dissatisfaction. Again, the contradictions of the *Maya* and *Avidya* doctrine often become acute. We may assert with great philosophic boldness that the world is an illusion, but we immediately find that this illusion itself requires explanation. We are on the horns of the dilemma of holding either that Nescience is purely negative, in which case it can produce nothing, not even an illusion; or, that it is a real originating principle, in which case that which it produces cannot be wholly an illusion. The dilemma is an uncomfortable one, and we extricate ourselves from it by a return to the world of experience.

The use of contradictory predicates, to which we have already referred, is another sign of uneasiness. They represent a more or less unsuccessful attempt to bring the Self into relation with the more concrete world of experience, and indicate a certain amount of dissatisfaction with the idea that we get nearer reality when we have to hold our peace and say nothing. We are not content to deny--we must also affirm. If there is an uncomfortable collision between the denial and the affirmation, this is without doubt unfortunate, but we must just submit to it, and hold the contradictory predicates together in our minds as peacefully as possible until better times come for thought. In the meantime, even if we can speak only with contradictions, yet it is better to speak than to remain silent. We must give *some* value to the world of experience, to the great world to which we ordinarily apply the term nature, even if this assignment of value conflicts with certain accepted principles of our philosophy. By much philosophical reasoning, *e.g.*, we may reach the position that reality is all a construction of the mind, shut up within the cavity of the heart. But yet we feel that this is not adequate, and so we think of the Universal Self as far out beyond our own self, penetrating and pervading all things through the boundless spaces of the world. We are lonely in the midst of our denials, and we wish they were not so necessary. Perhaps here we may have reached the inner spirit of *Chhandogya Upanishad* III, 14, 3, " This is my soul in my heart, smaller than rice-corn or barley-corn or mustard seed. This is my soul, greater than the heaven, greater than the worlds."

Again, we attribute the same feeling of loneliness to the divine Self with whom we are in communion, only the feeling now becomes a causal world-principle and not simply distress of soul. Perhaps this mood may underlie another famous passage in the *Chhandogya* VI, 2, 3—" In the beginning there was that only which is one only, without a second. . . . . It thought, may I be many, may I go forth,"—and then the process of going forth is described: the world is reached again and the ordinary experience of mankind is rehabilitated.

The problem at once arises as to how we may re-establish this world and at the same time retain something of the character of the idealistic position.

Here comes in the use of symbols and metaphors with their double advantage. They imply a recognition of the world of ordinary experience, just as language implies the recognition of other persons with whom we may speak. At the same time, being merely words and pictures, "names and forms," they do not commit the philosopher to a full admission of the reality of the world of sense. If the vulgar crowd mistake the purpose of the signs, and attribute to them a reality which they do not possess, the philosopher is not responsible for this, nor for the acknowledged consequence that "symbols in the hands of the multitude very readily become idols."[1]

It is impossible to find any symbol which does not implicitly admit the reality of the finite world. We have already considered the realistic implications of the metaphor of rivers running into the sea. But the same impression of veiled admission of the reality of the finite is produced by other metaphors which are perhaps more closely illustrative of the movement of thought we are considering. One of the most favourite metaphors is that of *salt*. The application of this metaphor occupies a whole section in the *Chhandogya Upanishad* (*viz.*, VI, 13). The disciple is told to throw salt into the water and then wait until the morning. In the morning he is sent again to the water, and is told to taste it in every part. On the surface, in the middle, and at the bottom he finds it salt—there is no part of it which is not salt. So the lesson of the all-pervasive character of Brahman is taught, and at the same time it *is admitted that there is a world for Brahman to pervade*. The water which the salt modifies is an actuality, otherwise the salt would not modify it. Similarly, the world which Brahman pervades is an actuality, otherwise Brahman could not pervade it. The simile in *Brihadaranyaka Upanishad* 1, 4, 7, is on much the same lines. There Brahman is said to enter into the world to the very tips of the finger nails, as a razor might be fitted into a razor case.

[1] Deussen, *Philosophy of the Upanishads*, p. 93.

It is true, of course, that other metaphors are more in accordance with negative teaching as to the unreality of the world. Finite things, *e.g.*, are compared to the sparks which fly from a central fire. As sparks rise and gleam and fade away in the darkness, so do the finite things of the world reveal themselves to our senses but for a moment and then fade away for ever. "As sparks come forth from fire, thus do all senses, all worlds, all Devas, all beings come forth from that central Self."[1] The same idea underlies the symbol of the crystal upon which the colours come and go, but which alone remains the permanent reality. Still, even in this group of figures, the implicit admission is obvious. Sparks and colours have at least a subordinate reality, so that the illustrations are not wholly consistent with the denial of the reality of the finite world.

The purpose of other symbols seems to be to emphasise the monistic and properly pantheistic character of the universe. It must be distinctly shown that the things of the finite world have no other source than Brahman. All doctrines of the creation of the world out of an extraneous matter must be opposed. Everything must come from Brahman, just as a spider spins its web out of its own body.[2] Further, the process is to be regarded as necessary throughout. There is little creative determination or choice on the part of Brahman. Things are sometimes described as springing from him in as natural and inevitable a way as the hairs spring out of the head of a man.

So, by means of these symbols, we get the conception of a graduated series of emanations from Brahman. Emanation takes the place of identity. The divine unity is laid hold of by the conditions of time, and becomes a process, conceived of, as a rule, in a pantheistic manner, and maintaining throughout its unity with the one divine source.

This process may be conceived of further from the point of view of its reconciliation with mythological

---

[1] Cf. *Brih. Up.* II, 1, 20. [2] Cf. *Brih. Up.* II, 1, 20.

ideas, and its adjustment to a system of cosmogonical deities and forces. Certain relics of ritual practices are used as symbols, and directions for sacrificial procedure are transformed into descriptions of cosmological development. The transference between ritual and cosmology is not always direct. The ritual is sometimes spiritualised, or, at least, becomes a procedure in the body of the worshipper instead of remaining as a manipulation of external things. It is thus brought at least one step nearer the point at which the individual self may be indentified with the self of the universe. The sacrifice, *e.g.*, which originally consisted in the pouring of milk into the fire, is transformed into the inspiration and expiration of breath, *i.e.*, the fire of the *Prana* is substituted for the actual fire. The sacrificial rite is thus brought into connection with the air which the individual and the universal share in common, and by virtue of this community obtains connection with a cosmical principle.[1] This is simply one illustration, amongst many, showing the possibility of adjustment between ritual and cosmology, but not necessarily giving us the order of procedure followed in other cases.

The actual stages of the process of emanation, theologically considered, correspond roughly to the three stages of waking consciousness, dreams, and dreamless sleep, through which the individual attains unity with Brahman. The cosmogony consists in a reversal of the order of the subjective stages of the soul's ascent, and a transference of these stages from the psychological to the cosmological sphere. To every subjective stage we have a corresponding cosmical stage, by which an objective explanation is offered of the experiences which the individual may have at that particular stage.

The neuter Brahma, the unmanifested, becomes the masculine Brahman. By a slightly more advanced determination this becomes equivalent to *Isvara*, or *Parameswar*, sometimes called the Karana Brahman, in which Brahman is said to assume the cosmic causal

[1] Cf. *Kaushitaki Up*. V, 3, 1.

body. At this stage he corresponds to, or sums up, the experiences of dreamless sleep. He is a universal spirit or Demiurge, described in the *Brihadaranyaka Up.* as dwelling in and actuating the earth, water, fire, air—in fact all living things and all minds, remaining unseen, unknown, unthought upon. He is not to be conceived theistically to any extent, as an objective deity having the individuality which could call forth worship. He is simply a stage in evolution, an impersonal spirit, pervading all things. If we connect with this conception the ideas of Maya and Avidya, we may regard Isvara as "the first figment of the world-fiction," whose unreality will, at the close of the age, be rediscovered and acted upon, and who will thus be reabsorbed in the characterless Brahman.

To the sum of dreaming consciousnesses corresponds *Hiranyagarbha*, germ of gold, under which form Brahman assumes the "cosmic subtle body." This form makes the first stage of individualisation possible—that individualisation which consists in separate mental action, but which has not yet reached concrete embodiment in material form. Hiranyagarbha is sometimes described as the Karya Brahman, the effect-god, the conscious totality of all effects. To the stage of waking-life corresponds *Vaisvanara* or *Viraj*—the "cosmic gross body," the power which gives unity to the bodily individualities making up the world.

The devolution of Brahman is treated from a less mythological and more physical point of view in the comparison with vital breath, as found both in the individual and the universe. Thus we have the twin conceptions of Prana and Vayu, the breath of the body being paralleled by the god of the wind. Another pair of conceptions is constituted by *Manas*, the mind, and *Akasa*, the ether. Brahman is to be worshipped under both these symbols, and thus an attempt is made to give a more psychical aspect to the manifestation of Brahman. The chief source for this conception is *Chhandogya* III, 18. It is difficult at first sight to see the connection between *Manas* and *Akasa*, unless we are to regard *Akasa* as equivalent simply to space, and, therefore, as the sphere in which objects appear to the manas. From this it would be but a short step to the conception of the one Being as manifested both in the world and in space.

There are many other symbols into the consideration of which we need not enter. One further point of interest may, however, be noted. There are certain passages in which generalised, intermediate, and semi-mythological conceptions are brought into connection with the elements as known to the physicists, or, in some cases, are entirely dispensed with. Brahman is regarded as producing directly the elements which, when brought under names and forms, make up the sum-total of cognisable reality. If any one of the ordinary elements are to be regarded as fundamental this place might be claimed by water.[1] But usually three or even five elements are mentioned.[2] Thus the material elements are provided for, and may be further developed through the principle of individuation, assuming specific forms with qualities capable of designation by means of a name.[3]

We have thus described the various aspects of the process by which in the Upanishads an attempt is made to give value to our ordinary experience, and to move from abstract idealism in a genuinely positive pantheistic direction. Or—to use more accurate terminology—we have traced the passing of negative into positive pantheism, or at least the oscillation between them. The monism of the system is, as we have seen, steadily maintained. There is no admission of an alien material out of which the world could be fashioned—everything comes from Brahman himself. And he pervades everything as an immanent principle—"he enters up to the finger tips." "Who'er beholds all living creatures as in him, and him the universal spirit as in all, henceforth regards no creature with contempt."[4] Into him everything returns at the end

---

[1] Cf. *Brih. Up.* I, 2, 2. [2] Cf. *Chhand. Up.* VI, 2, 3 ; *Pras. Up.* IV, 8. [3] Cf. *Brih. Up.* I, 1, 7. [4] Cf. also *Isa Up.*

of the age. Thus the whole process has a three-fold aspect—origination, growth, dissolution. "That from whence these beings are born, that by which when born they live, that into which they enter at their death, this is Brahman."[1] As has been said, the original identity is laid hold of by the conditions of time, but the plurality into which it is thus developed is a plurality within a unity. Origination, development, dissolution are all phases of the One.

We have thus presented the two phases of the teaching of the *Upanishads*. We shall not enter any more fully than we have done in a previous chapter into the vexed question as to which phase is to be regarded as the more authoritative of the two. A discussion of this difficulty would involve a reference to the whole controversy between Sankara and Ramanuja, into which controversy limits of space forbid our entering. We shall be content with leaving the two phases side by side, indicating only that the tendency seems to be rather in the negative direction. There are indications that the world process which has just been described is not to be taken veiy seriously. There are, *e.g.*, forced attempts at identification of the various stages of the process, as if the identity had to be preserved at all costs. Again, only a small portion of the original Brahman enters into the process. There is an infinite reserve, and this gives us the idea that creation is of subordinate importance. Sankara holds that the same depreciation is involved in the conflicting statements which are given of the process of creation. The confusion indicates according to him a certain amount of indifference. It is not worth while attaining consistency on a matter of such slight importance. A similar impression is produced by the assertion that creation is simply the sport of Brahman. This may indicate merely failure to provide an explanation, but it may also contain a slight hint of the small importance of the world for which explanation is required. Further, the process has no ultimate meaning. At the end of the age there

---

[1] Cf. *Taitt. Up.* III, 3, 1.

is the return of all things into the original unity, when all things will be as they were in the beginning. Unity has conquered along the greater part of the battle line. However, we need not emphasise unduly the victory, having regard to the strength of the combatants on both sides. We shall proceed to the further question as to whether we may sum up our analysis of the two phases by bringing both under the head of pantheism.

The fundamental formula of pantheism would seem to be a double one—*nothing is which is not God, and God is everything which is.* There can be no other source of being than God, and no other power than His. We and the rest of the universe are but phases of His Being, and nothing can be conceived as having even temporary separation from Him. God and the Universe must be identified, and if any part of the universe cannot be identified with Him, that part must be negated.

Now, though it is not pretended that there is nothing but pantheism in the Upanishads, it may with confidence be asserted that the non-pantheistic elements are not predominant, and, conversely, it may be said that the fundamental tendency is to regard God as the sole reality. No difficulty has arisen about the identification of reality and God, the difficulty has rather been about the extent of the reality which is thus to be identified. In other words, the difficulty is not about whether all is God, but about whether God is all? Is emphasis to be laid upon the world or God? Are we to be positive or negative in our attitude?

Here we find the explanation of the hesitation which exists in the minds of some about the propriety of applying the word pantheism to the teaching of the Upanishads. The general pantheistic formula is capable of a double interpretation, and, in thinking of pantheism, philosophers have had now one and now the other interpretation more prominently in their minds. We have seen, also, that the teaching of the Upanishads is capable of a similarly double interpretation. Consequently, the application to this teaching of the word pantheism will vary, both according to the general idea of pantheism which is in the mind of the writer and according to the particular interpretation of the Upanishads which he has adopted.

If one, *e.g.*, holds a naturalistic doctrine of pantheism and adopts an idealistic interpretation of the Upanishads, the difficulty of employing the word pantheism will be at its maximum. It must, however, be confessed that this difficulty is greater with the negative phase of the teaching of the Upanishads than with the positive. In this double reference most people would agree with the statement that "each Upanishad inculcates a pantheism of one sort or another," or, with the assertion of Cowell, that "through all the Upanishads there runs an unmistakeable spirit of pantheism." The monism of the system is undoubtedly strong. It has, indeed, been objected that this positive phase goes so far in the direction of concession to the empirical point of view as to lose hold upon pantheistic unity. It is said that the hierarchies of divine beings, or—more generally—the cosmogonies of the Upanishads suggest the idea of the derivation of the world from a being who does not pass over into the world, but remains one, indivisible and transcendent. In other words, it is asserted that there are theistic elements in the system, and that we have at least an approach towards these in the conceptions of the neuter Brahma taking the masculine form Brahman, and by a still further determination becoming Isvara or Parameswar. It is alleged that wherever description of a deity is possible, so that he may become an object of worship, and this deity is still conceived of as one and as the source of all things—there we have theism as distinct from pantheism on the one hand and polytheism on the other. There is a hint of a theistic religious relationship in *Mundaka* III, 2, 1, where the idea of worship is emphasised; and the idea of worshipful gazing upon a divine object also appears in *Svetasvatara* IV, 7. There are traces of theistic independence and transcendence in such passages as *Isa*, 8, "He is a seer, wise, omnipotent, self-existent, he disposed all things rightly for eternal years," and in *Katha* V, 13, "There is one eternal thinker, thinking non-eternal thoughts, who, though one, fulfils the desires of many."

Still these passages do not seem to succeed in establishing a fully theistic position. However clearly the attitude of true worship may seem to be indicated, there is a constant refrain, sometimes even in the same verse, to the effect that the Self who is to be worshipped is the self of the worshipper, and that, consequently, there is no such distinction between the two as is demanded by the fully theistic relation. We must not be misled by phrases such as "God is in man," or "he is within the self." The "in" here suggests identity rather than communion.

Further, the independence of God which is sometimes ascribed to the world is of the most temporary character. The world-process is a process of unfolding and retraction from the *pralaya* state, in which there is no difference of name and form, into the world of ordinary qualities, and back again, at the end of a *kalpa*, to the same state. Again, the independence is not only temporary, it is also extremely partial. The world is separated from God, according to the teaching of the *Mandukya Upanishad*, only as the beams which stream forth from the sun. Difference may be allowed, but the difference is kept strictly within the bounds of unity. The creature is not an emanation external to God, but always merely "a finite mode of infinite being."

The Indian doctrine of creation is not that which we usually associate with theism, and which includes the ideas of free choice and self-limitation on the part of God. It is rather a necessary unfolding on the part of God. If there is a wish at all, it is of an exceedingly elementary kind. We have, indeed, the words, "Let me be many, let me go forth," but immediately, as it were, the creative impulse dies away and its place is taken by a natural process of evolution or devolution. The word *srishti* means a discharge, a setting free, an emission, an emergence of the universe from Brahman. If it is creation at all, it is creation in the Spinozistic sense, a process from which all freedom (in the ordinary meaning of the word) and all purpose have been excluded, which is deterministic in its origin and deterministic in its working. There is, further, no idea of such limitation on the part of God as could give rise to an independent world, containing not only created beings but also *creators*, capable of affirming their reality. The idea of creation, which we find in the Upanishads, is one which dates from Vedic literature, where we read that Prajapati did not create a world but simply transformed himself and his different members into the regions of the universe. The idea has not changed during the intervening centuries, and is indeed so different from our usual idea of creation that we might borrow a term from Deussen and call it cosmogonism rather than a process of creation.

We find then that the theistic elements in the positive form of the teaching of the Upanishads are comparatively few, and are unable to detach themselves to any extent from the surrounding pantheism, by which term we may quite adequately describe the system so far as we have considered it.

Serious objection has, however, been taken to the application of the term to the negative aspect of the system. A writer in *East and West*, April, 1911, says about the Vedanta generally: "The Vedantist does not say that 'All is God,' but that 'God is All,' which is a very different position. His meaning is that *God alone is*, and that of nothing else can it be asserted that it *is*. The All of the Pantheist does not exist for the Vedantist at all: it simply does not really exist. This God is not immanent in the universe, for the universe does not exist. This philosophy is clearly not pantheism. It is transcendentalism of the most extreme type, and for transcendentalism there is no place in pantheism."

In regard to this argument we may say that it does not seem to matter so much, after all, whether we say that "All is God" or "God is All." Both are pantheistic, the first admittedly so, and the second by implication. Before we can say "God alone exists," we must have some conception of that of which we are positing reality.[1] It must represent an All for us. We are asserting that nothing which is not God exists, which is very nearly the same as to say that whatever is not excluded from God and may be identified with God exists—"whatever is, is the Atman." In short, we have good reason to think that there is no insuperable objection to simple conversion of the proposition, "God is All" into "All is God." If you have, that is, only one reality, and are inclined, notwithstanding its vagueness, to call this reality God, there is no valid reason why the system should not be called pantheism. The two positions indicated by the double formula, "God is all that is," and "all that is is God," are historically, psychologically, and logically bound up together. In relation to our particular problem we may put the formula alongside the statement in the *Brihadaranyaka Up.* II, 4, 5, "With the knowledge of the Atman all is known, and we may see that this is susceptible of two interpretations—either (1) apart from the Atman there is nothing else to be known"; or (2) in the knowledge of the Atman we have the key to all other knowledge. The two interpretations are inextricably bound up together. Psychologically it is simply a question of whether the key will turn or not. If the philosopher finds the key difficult to turn, *i.e.*, if he cannot discover a satisfactory relation between the particularity of the world and the Being of God, he may adopt the shorthand method of negating the world altogether. It is true that he thus reaches what, from one point of view, might be called an idealistic position, but he does not cease to be a pantheist; for after all he is concerned more with the reality of the result than with the ideality of the method by which it has been reached, and his attitude is intended to be more religious than philosophical. It is a positive statement which his soul makes—the *All* for him is God. Ideal-

[1] Cf. Bergson's discussion of the impossibility of pure negation in *Creative Evolution*.

ism is the method by which the ultimate pantheistic unity is gained, and it is a method which is necessitated by the requirement that in order to be thoroughly pantheistic in his experience the individual must be able to identify his own essential self with God, and must be at liberty to deny everything which makes it difficult to bring about this identification. We may hold, therefore, to Mr. Allanson Picton's definition of pantheism, as a system which "absolutely identifies God and the Universe, so that there cannot be anything but God," and may conclude that this definition can be appropriately applied to both aspects of the teaching of the Upanishads.

Having thus gathered together the essential characteristics of the teaching, we are now in a position to investigate the effects which this teaching has upon our sense of the value of life. In a word, is this teaching optimistic or pessimistic in its influence? We are not now dealing with a vague intellectual *milieu*, but with a definite attitude to life which seems inseparable from the philosophy which has been adopted.

The life from which we have to escape is painted by the teachers of the Upanishads in prevailingly sombre hue. We may call to mind the stages by which we reach the highest life, and reflect that both waking life and dreamless sleep are conditions of discomfort and even of misery. The earthly life is that from which we essentially need deliverance, and the aim seems to be, therefore, to present this life in such a way that the need will be felt in the acutest possible manner. Existence is more or less of a curse, and the question seems always on the point of being raised—Why any Being should have been so unwise or so indifferent to consequences as to produce such a state of things?

We find this sense of disgust, this feeling of the futility, impermanence and misery of all mundane things, expressed most clearly in the *Maitrayana Upanishad* IV, v. 3ff. We give Monier Williams' verse translation—

"In this decaying body, made of bones,
Skin, tendons, membranes, muscles, blood, saliva,

Full of putrescence and impurity,
What relish can there be for true enjoyment?
In this weak body, ever liable
To wrath, ambition, avarice, illusion,
To fear, grief, envy, separation
From those we hold most dear, association
With those we hate, continually exposed
To hunger, thirst, disease, decrepitude,
Emanation, growth, decline and death,
What relish can there be for true enjoyment?
The universe is tending to decay,
Grass, trees and animals spring up and die;
But what are they? Earth's mighty men are gone,
Leaving their joys and glories all."

All the elements of pessimism are here, disgust at particular objects, dissatisfaction with the general scheme of things, their vicissitudes and their impermanence, a sense of constraint and an unquiet yearning for release. The passage concludes with a quaint comparison of the worshipper to a frog at the bottom of a dry well—and the supplication, "Deign to rescue me (literally, take me out): Thou art our only refuge, Holy Lord." And as we read the passage as a whole, we conclude that the well is very dry, its sides very lofty, and the frog very helpless.

We have already referred to the loneliness of Brahman as one of the motives for the evolution of the world. We might also have referred to the conception of *tapas*, which, upon investigation, yields the idea that creation is essentially an act of self-renunciation on the part of Brahman, involving labour, fatigue and pain. We refer to it here because this conception seems to involve an explicit judgment of pessimism passed on the world as a whole. The idea is not very far distant that the whole process is not altogether desirable. We may say more generally, and less metaphysically, that the whole ascetic ideal is a depreciatory judgment upon the world, from which world ascetic practices are intended to secure deliverance.

Now, very little attempt is made by either Indian or European writers to deny the sombre character of the picture of ordinary life which is given us in the Upanishads, but many of them protest most vigorously against the suggestion that the system as a whole is to be labelled pessimistic. It is unlikely that a protest so generally made is wholly without warrant. Max Müller emphasises the point that the misery is always to be viewed in relation to the deliverance, and argues that a philosophy which promises deliverance cannot be called pessimistic. Deussen follows much the same line of defence. He points out that the pessimistic view of life which may be detected in the Upanishads is a presupposition of the doctrine of deliverance, and that, in thus emphasising the gloom of the state from which we must escape, the philosophy of the Upanishads is in no way different from the philosophy of other religions. In particular it may be paralleled in Christian doctrine : the pilgrim sets out from a City of Destruction.

We must, of course, take account of the promise of deliverance, but we must at the same time remember that a promise by itself is not enough. We must also have a reasonable hope of fulfilment, and this hope in its fulness will depend upon an affirmative answer to two questions—(1) whether the promised deliverance is possible ; (2) whether, even if possible, it is a deliverance worth struggling for.

We shall consider the second of these questions first. Our aim will be to discover whether the ultimate state of the delivered soul, as described in the Upanishads, is properly regarded as a state of happiness or bliss. Of course, our argument will not attempt to show that it is happiness in the sense of being the satisfaction of ordinary desires of a material kind. It is rather a higher happiness we have in view, a happiness which might be otherwise called blessedness or bliss. It would be well that this distinction should be kept in mind, for any accusation of pessimism is often met by the suggesting that the critics are merely disappointed in the hope of happiness of a lower kind—the kind of happiness indicated by the popular Indian phrase, the "fruit of works."

It must be admitted that, over and over again, in the Upanishads the ultimate state is described as a state of *bliss.* Some of the most beautiful passages in the Upanishads are devoted to the strengthening of this expectation. The *anandamaya* state is the highest, and this is a state of bliss. Bliss is not only a quality of Brahman, but his very essence, and the devout worshipper who has reached the goal participates in this essence. "The infinite is bliss. There is no bliss in anything finite. Infinity only is bliss."[1] By means of union with Brahman we obtain the benefit of deliverance and of absolute spiritual satisfaction. The idea of deliverance is emphasised in *Chhandogya* VII, 1, 6: "Those who depart from here, after having discovered the Self and those true desires, for them there is freedom in all the worlds." The positive aspect of satisfaction is described in innumerable passages. The end is compared to hidden treasure in *Chhandogya* VIII, 3-2, and, in less metaphorical language, we are told in the same Upanishad that from the Self, as obtained by the worshipper, spring hope, memory, understanding (Cf. *Chhandogya* VII, 26-1). All disabilities are left behind. "Therefore, he who has crossed that bank (which separates him from Brahman), if he is blind, ceases to be blind; if wounded, ceases to be wounded; if afflicted, ceases to be afflicted."[2] In the *Taittiriya Upanishad* a long list of other possible modes of life are given, and the bliss of the enlightened man is said, in every case, to be a hundred times greater and fuller than the bliss which would be obtained from any other source. We are given the description of a "noble young man, firm and strong, for whom the whole world is full of wealth." Yet his bliss is exceeded a hundred times by the bliss of the human genii, and their bliss again by the bliss of the Divine genii, and so on, through an ascending scale and constant hundred-fold multiplication, until we reach the bliss of the Devas, the bliss of Indra, of Brihaspati, of Prajapati, and finally the bliss of Brahman, which exceeds by a hundred times the bliss of the highest beneath him. The climax which concerns us, is that this bliss of Brahman may also be enjoyed by the "great sage who is free from desires."

[1] Cf. *Chhandogya* VII, 23, 1. [2] *Chhandogya* VII, 4, 2.

Sometimes it is frankly admitted that this bliss is indescribable. "Who by reflection of the purified spirit, sinks into the self, experiences happiness which no words can describe, but which may be experienced in the inner heart."[1] When, however, attempts at description are made, one of the favourite figures is the contrast between night and day, together with the beauty of the everlasting light, suggestive of many New Testament passages. Brahman himself is light, and the light shines upon the faces of the worshippers (Cf. also *Chhandogya* III, 11, 3). "To him who thus knows the Brahma Upanishad, the sun does not rise and does not set. For him there is day, once for all." The effect upon the worshipper is described in IV, 14, 2: "Your face shines like one who knows Brahman."

The idea of satisfaction with wisdom is introduced into a very comprehensive passage in the *Mundaka Upanishad* III, 2, 5, which also combines both the negative and the positive aspects of the promised bliss. "The sages are *satisfied with wisdom*. Their true self is manifested, their attachment ceases and they become tranquil. Obtaining the Omnipresent everywhere, these wise men will enter into him." There is a somewhat similar passage in *Mandukya*, 47, where those who have true wisdom are said to describe the highest as "free, peaceful, passionless, the abode of indescribable intensity of bliss, eternal and eternally conscious of eternal objects," and it must be remembered that this ultimate is also the goal of all their striving.

Yet we still ask the question, Is this tranquil bliss—a bliss of absorption rather than communion—ultimately satisfying? To many minds it presents itself as negative and abstract. It consists in a turning away from all activities and experience of ordinary life, and its content is hardly more describable than that of the absolute to whom or to which only negative predicates may be applied. One cannot get away from the idea that the bliss which is promised us is something of the nature of a soporific. It is the deadening down of

[1] Cf. *Maitrayana* VI, 34.

activity. It is the resultant of many artificial measures including, *e.g.*, the repetition of the syllable *Om*, which is intended to bring us into the proper condition of concentration or one-pointedness. It is the culmination of a series of processes by which we divest ourselves of the sheaths of ordinary life, and fling them from us as garments that are outworn. One cannot get away from the feeling that it is of the nature of a soporific. It is, indeed, explicitly compared to deep sleep in which our desires stand still and all our strivings cease.

Of course the necessity of the negative movement in the moral and spiritual life must be admitted. There must be opposition to the lower forms of life if the soul is to live; but this does not mean that the higher life must itself be negative. Both aspects of the matter are brought out by George Eliot in the famous passage in *Romola*: "One can only have the highest happiness—such as goes along with being a great man—by having wide thought and much feeling for the rest of the world, as well as for ourselves; and this sort of happiness often brings so much pain with it that we can only tell it from pain by its being what we would choose before anything else, because our souls see that it is good." The distinction between the higher happiness and the lower happiness is put in this passage almost with the strength of paradox, but the positive character of the higher life is also clearly indicated. It must consist not in an annihilation, but in a transformation of the lower. It is a bliss which consists in the strengthening of all true desire, in width of thought and sympathy. There is no emptiness of negation, but a positive carrying out of the essential choice of the soul.

It would seem that the distinction between higher and lower happiness has been to a great extent forgotten by the Upanishads. In their anxiety to withdraw the thoughts of men from lower and materialistic rewards, they have dispensed with that high and spiritual reward which consists in the increase of the strength of the soul—the "wages of going on," as Tennyson would put it. They have been so anxious to dissociate themselves from those who seek after a heaven of more or less material bliss, that they have gone to the opposite extreme and conceived of an ideal state which is the negation of all desire, an eternal life of passive enjoyment without sufficient character to preserve even the individuality of the soul. The house of the soul has been swept and garnished, purified of everything that is earthly, but mere sweeping and garnishing does not ensure that heavenly guests shall take the place of the earthly. And until these heavenly guests come in there is no bliss in the true sense of the word. There may be quietness, but it is the quietness of death.

Of course we may be referred to such passages as *Chhandogya* VIII, 1, 6, which describes the state of bliss in a more positive way, and speaks of "discovering the self and those true desires." This passage, Max Müller interprets as referring to desires "which we ought to have, the fulfilment of which depends entirely upon ourselves." This does not help us very much in the discovery of a positive content for the Self. It is essentially a Stoic attitude, and its tendency is entirely negative. For there are, properly speaking, no desires which depend entirely upon ourselves. In its very nature desire implies a going forth beyond ourselves. To restrict ourselves to desires which depend entirely on ourselves very soon comes to mean the annihilation of desire. If we are so self-sufficient in our desires, there is a danger that we may soon come to desire nothing at all. We demand a connection with the universal by positive affirmation, if we are to have security of bliss.

The promise of bliss in the Upanishads includes no crowning of life's blessedness, no transformation of the joys of earth into the joys of heaven, no return to earth of the transfigured soul. The break with ordinary experience is abrupt and complete. We find a mournfully ascetic tone in the *Katha Upanishad* II, 6, 12, "When all desires that dwell in the heart cease, then the mortal becomes immortal," and again, three verses further on, "When all the ties of the heart are severed here on earth, then the mortal becomes immortal." The bliss we are to strive for is the result of abstraction wholly negative. We cannot describe it except by saying that it is not the happiness of ordinary life. In the *Katha Upanishad* II, 12, we read, further, "Having recognised, by the knowledge obtained through spiritual abstraction, that Divine being who is difficult to be seen, who is hidden, who pervades all things, who is in the heart, who lives in inaccessible places—the wise man gives up both joy and sorrow." Not only the sorrows but also the joys of life, however pure these latter may be, have to be entirely left behind. And yet the teachers of this ideal in no way forgo their claim to describe it as bliss. Can we say that this claim is justified? Does it not, on the contrary, seem necessary to say that any bliss which is to maintain its attraction must justify the impulses which are essential to human nature? If it cannot do this, then a reaction in the direction of pessimism is inevitable. The bliss may seem, indeed, to be obtained occasionally in the rare moments of philosophic abstraction, but it is without content and without security amidst the ordinary experiences of life. The ideal set before us does not allow free play to human activity, and this unexercised activity reacts upon the mind of the worshipper, and produces a sense of bafflement and disappointment. The bliss has been purchased at the expense of human experience and activity, and yet it does not provide for any higher exercise. So the price which has been paid for it comes to be regarded as excessive. Men are apt to pass on to the judgment that, if happiness is not to be found in the ordinary world, it is not to be found anywhere, and they are especially likely to pass this judgment, if the happiness which is offered them outside of human experience is of so vague and shadowy a character as that which is described in the Upanishads.

Further, if an ideal is to maintain its attraction, it must be a support amidst the sorrows of the temporal order. If it cannot afford this support, the sorrows of ordinary life become all the more overwhelming. It may be said, indeed, that the negative ideal teaches us the unimportance of all ordinary sorrows, and so engenders an imperturbable Stoic attitude. But, in the first place, it seems almost a misuse of terms to describe such an attitude as productive of bliss, and, in the second place, the Stoical attitude is admittedly most difficult to maintain. The reason of this difficulty is that it can say only that nothing matters. It cannot make the further statement, that, though nothing matters in one sphere, something *does* matter in another and higher sphere. A morally disconcerting positive can be satisfactorily met only by another positive—this time of a morally stimulating character. The morally disconcerting positive we are here concerned with is the fact of human sorrow, and it can be dealt with only by a bliss which is positive, and is not merely a contempt for human sorrow, but a purification of it from everything that is degrading and a transformation of it into joy. It must be remembered, also, that a special duty in dealing with human sorrow is laid upon the teachers of the Upanishad. They have painted ordinary life in such sombre colours that the light of the bliss which they promise requires to be all the stronger in order that it may brighten the gloom. They have not hesitated to point out the evils of the actual: therefore the demand becomes all the more urgent that they should bring with them a remedy for these evils. They cannot be said to have met this demand. They have told us that everything outside of Brahman is misery, but they have left us only with a negative and abstract Brahman, so that the practical conclusion is that everything is misery. The result of the failure would seem to be that men continue hopeless in the midst of the troubles of their ordinary life, or pursue the fitful pleasures of that life until satiety brings disappointment.

We have shown that the bliss which is promised in the Upanishads is a bliss which is hardly worth having, and have thus answered our first question in the negative. We cannot altogether thrust out of our conception of life the idea of happiness in the form of satisfaction of the highest elements in our nature. In drawing attention to this inadequacy in the Upanishad ideal we have already answered, by implication, the second of our questions—Is the ideal attainable? Now the Upanishads appear to be so much concerned with opposition to the lower kind of happiness, that they pay little attention to the means by which even such bliss as they retain in their conception may be attained. This bliss cannot be called happiness in the sense of positive fulfilment: consequently it does not call forth energy in the struggle. As Eucken says, "It is a thing to be insisted on, that man should let the thought of happiness control his efforts, for it is only by doing so that he can put all the vigour of the strength of his emotions into his action. He cannot devote all his energies to the struggle after anything from which he does not expect to find satisfaction for his own nature."[1]

Ends in human life can be attained only by desire for them. But in the ideal as described in the Upanishads, desire has been excluded. Therefore, the end is unattainable, the bliss is out of reach. Joy is promised to the soul which has won deliverance, but the means of attaining that deliverance have been denied him, and so joy turns to bitterness, and optimism to pessimism.

Further, bliss is itself relative to desire. It is that which is desired, and it can be attained only through desire. But desire is a sin: therefore the end as gained is the result of an action which ought to have been condemned. Thus the successful devotee will always be haunted by the consciousness that he has gained a good end by evil means, and his bliss will fall short of completeness.

Thus we are compelled to answer in the negative the two questions with which we started. No satisfactory means are provided for reaching the bliss which is promised; and, even if it could be attained, it would not commend itself as adequate. This conclusion is supported by judgments which Indian commentators

---

[1] *Problem of Human Life*, p. 337.

have themselves passed upon the coldness and futility of the prevailingly negative teaching. Ramanuja says, in his Commentary, II, 3, 42: "Truly if such were the teaching of the Vedas, what more would the Veda be than the idle talk of a person out of his mind?" and such a passage hardly indicates contentment with the prevailing view. There is also a revolt against the loss of personal existence, which is an implication never far away from the teaching of the Upanishads. It is felt to be too big a price to pay. As Ramanuja again says, "A man who, suffering pain, mental or other kind, naturally begins to reflect how he may once for all free himself from all the manifold afflictions and enjoy a state of untroubled ease, the desire for final release having thus arisen in him, he at once sets to work to accomplish it. If, on the other hand, he were to realise that the effect of such activity would be the loss of personal existence, he surely would turn away as soon as somebody began to tell him about release. And the result of this would be, that in the absence of willing and qualified pupils the whole scriptural teaching as to final release would lose its authoritativeness. No sensible person exerts himself under the influence of the idea that after he himself has perished there will remain some entity called "pure light" (Ramanuja, Vol. I, p. 70). The defects which have been pointed out by Ramanuja, and which he himself has not been able entirely to remove, are inseparable from the teaching of the Upanishads. The verdict of history has emphasised the same defects. The teaching has failed to satisfy the human heart. The ideal is empty, abstract and alien, and so the influence of it is on the whole in the direction of pessimism. Into the causes of this pessimism we shall enquire more fully in the next two chapters, and the concluding chapter will suggest where a remedy may be found.

CHAPTER IV

The Intellectualism of the Upanishads and Their Metaphysical Inadequacy

IN the preceding chapter we came to the general conclusion that the ideal set forth in the Upanishads is of too abstract a character to satisfy the needs of men. We shall now enquire further into the nature and the causes of this failure.

Prominent amongst these causes is what might be called the *excessive intellectualism* of the system. It places the whole, or, at least, the greater part, of the burden of deliverance upon the intellect, and crushes it with a weight which is too great for it to bear. There is little connection with practical interests and the emotional colouring is often very slight. Deliverance is to be gained by insight and not by action. As is said in the *Maitrayana Upanishad* VI, 34,11 : "Mind alone is the cause of bondage and liberty for men: if attached to the world it becomes bound: if free from the world, that is liberty." We might emphasise this point by contrast with the teaching of the Bible. It has been frequently said that while the Bible discovers depravity on the volitional side of human nature, the Upanishads discover it on the intellectual side. It is true that activity is allowed a certain amount of value in the Upanishads. There seems to be general agreement that works, and especially ritual works, are necessary as preliminaries (Cf. *Mundaka* III, 2, 10 and *Chhandogya* VII, 21, 1); but there is much greater uncertainty about whether works lead to the highest result and as to whether they are necessary for the permanence of this result. There is on the whole a disposition to confine them to the sphere of preliminaries, and to lay exclusive emphasis upon the contemplative aspect of the religious attitude. There could be no objection to this depreciation of merely *ritual* works, but danger arises when dislike of ritual works becomes dislike of all works whatsoever, and religion lapses into quietism. The tone of the *Katha Upanishad, e.g.*, is predominantly passive. The supreme condition of unity with the Divine is undisturbed contemplation, rather than rigorous righteousness of life and reconstructive zeal. The man who withdraws himself from all ordinary activities, whether ceremonial or social, and who gives himself up to the life of quiescent contemplation, has the best, and, indeed, according to some—the only chance of attaining that unity with Brahman which is the goal of the soul. "Cease from works," is an oft-recurring refrain in the Upanishads, and sometimes this advice has been but too readily followed. It would be unfair, however, not to point out that what might be called the inner aspect of moral activity—the necessity of sincerity and purity—has often been emphasised. But this inward condition of the soul is regarded rather as a means by which undisturbed intellectual contemplation may be attained than as itself the goal of religious endeavour. Generally speaking, the connection between thought and life is not maintained with sufficient closeness, and just on this account thought becomes, as we shall see,. somewhat shadowy and unreal.

Nor can it be said that the emotional element is strong in the Upanishads themselves. Though this element comes to its own, and more than its own, in later *bhakti* literature, yet this is due rather to a reaction from the prevailing teaching of the Upanishads than to a development out of it. The slightly warmer colouring of the *Brihadaranyaka Up.*, shown in such passages as, "A husband is loved for the love of the Self which is one within us all," indicates an emotional rapture which is on the whole rare in these writings. The bliss which is promised, as we have seen, is of an exceedingly rarified kind and almost entirely negative. It is a vacuity of feeling rather than a positive content. The prevailing doctrine is that the emotions belong to the lower region of the soul, and must be reckoned amongst the desires which have to be sacrificed before true deliverance is possible.

No doubt the teacher of the Upanishads, while admitting that he lays special emphasis upon the intellect, would protest that he is not thinking only of the purely logical or discursive intellect. He would claim rather that the intellect with which he is dealing is intuitive and has also a more comprehensive scope than the usual use of the term indicates. Is not the *anandamaya* stage, *e.g.*, put above the *jnanamaya*, and this again above the *manomaya?* This contention may be fully admitted, but it may be argued that no positive meaning is given in the system to the supra-intellectual or extra-intellectual elements, and they are left to borrow their character from the intellectual contemplation which induces them. Thus the mere presence of these vague elements does not relieve us from the necessity of dealing with the situation created by the strong emphasis upon the intellect alone. It will be found that the other elements come in rather as a result of the failure of the intellect to make good its claims than as a natural expansion of these claims. The burden upon the intellect is not *intentionally* lessened.

This emphasis upon the intellect is not peculiar to the Upanishads amongst systems of pantheism. There seems to be some essential connection between intellectualism and pantheism. Indeed, the former has sometimes been assigned as one of the causes of the acceptance of the latter. Prof. Upton, in his *Hibbert Lectures*, says, that the pantheism of the East is the inevitable result of intellectualism. So, if we have been correct in describing the philosophy of the Upanishads as pantheism, we shall naturally expect to find a clear strain of intellectualism in it. We shall expect to find that religion is more a form of knowledge than anything else and that the religious relation—if it can be properly called a relation—is one in which the soul of the worshipper is of one piece, as it were, with the God whom he worships. As in other pantheistic systems, it is by knowledge that the goal can be reached. The aim of the worshipper in the Upanishads is "to *recognise* his own self as a limited reflection of the highest, to *know* his Self as the highest Self, and *through that knowledge* to return to it, to regain his identity with it. Here to know was to be, *to know the Atman was to be the Atman*."[1]

Is this domination by intellectualism justified? The question is as yet quite general—is the intellect in its nature capable of performing the task allotted to it? The adequacy of the particular solution offered will be briefly referred to later.

Specialisation on intellectual lines undoubtedly carries with it a certain exaltation of mood—the thrill of the student in his study or the rapture of the recluse in his forest—but on the whole it is apt to produce a grey view of life. Contemplation in India especially belongs to the period of life when the active duties of the householder and citizen are dispensed with. It is, therefore, a practical illustration of Hegel's saying, that "The shades of evening have already fallen when the owl of Minerva takes her flight." Reality is apt to become stony and rigid. The movement of life escapes. It has often been pointed out recently that the method of the intellect is essentially static, and that it is incapable of dealing under its favourite mathematical and mechanical categories with movement and life. It thus allows a considerable part of reality to slip through the network of its system. As Eucken puts it, "It is only through connection with life that thought ceases to be abstract and becomes concrete. All philosophy and theory of knowledge which scorn this connection, and seek to base themselves upon reflective considerations and presumed necessities of thought, never go beyond the domain of shadows or reach pure reality."[2] We may say that also for some minds the reality with which thought can deal presents itself, not so much as a realm of grey shadows, but rather as a system of

[1] Max Müller, *Upanishads*, Vol. IX, p. 30.

[2] Art Knowledge and Life—*Philosophical Review*, January, 1913.

mechanical laws, creating the feeling of inexorable and oppressive necessity, which, however it may be resented, cannot be changed. We are restricted to the world as it is, and may not think of that which ought to be. We contemplate the actual without distinction of value of good or bad. If we are discontented with it, we are not encouraged to transform it, we can only abandon it. Thus we see that intellectualism has a close connection with the emancipation doctrine, and its implied judgment as to the hopelessness of the actual. As was the case later with Plotinus, all change is regarded as a degradation of reality, and thus the possibility of relief through change is closed to us. A depressing contrast is thus introduced between natural and normal human impulse and the nature of reality. We all know that the most effective way in which we may get rid of a melancholy mood is to go and do something, but such a remedy is rendered impossible in a system where action is despised. Intellectualism thus falls a ready prey to naturalism in which the processes of the universe are regarded as quite independent of any activity on our part. No room is left for progress, at least for such progress as is distinct from process and is the result of a conception of vocation. Naturalism is closely connected with intellectualism for the reason that the former, though it admits process, still takes a static view of the universe. The lines of development are determined from the beginning, and remain stationary throughout, and the end is as the beginning. The static and the cyclic are to all intents and purposes identical conceptions. Sometimes we may be contented with this asserted impossibility of effective and self-determined activity, but such contentment is rare and belongs to moods of absorbed contemplation, which are very frequently induced and still more frequently maintained by artificial means. As a rule we "claim to live in a world where things really happen, where our energies really count for something and determine something."[1]

[1] Inge, *Faith and Its Psyhology*, p. 195.

This inherent incapacity of thought, when taken alone, explains why the Ultimate Reality of the Upanishads so often borders on nothingness. Thought, when exclusively relied upon, overreaches itself and annihilates itself. The response of the human soul to the problem of the world can never be made wholly from the intellectual side. If an attempt is made thus to restrict the response, the inevitable result is an acute sense of failure, of confusion, of incapacity. And this depressing consequence is, to a large extent, independent of the internal coherency and logical success of the system which may be constructed by intellectual effort. It is rather a general sense of the futility of *all* merely intellectual constructions, however well put together they may be. It is a result of the overburdening of the intellectual faculties as such. Of course, if the particular construction should turn out to be metaphysically unsatisfactory this would supply an additional reason for depression, but it is at least conceivable that even a logically consistent construction might be a cause of pessimism, if it depends on the activity of the intellect alone.

Before we go on to offer a brief criticism of the particular metaphysics of the system, one or two other consequences of general intellectualism may be noted. An exclusive reliance upon intellect is apt to result in an exclusive attitude on the part of the philosopher towards his fellow men. After all, intellectual procedure is possible only for the select few, and if deliverance is dependent on this procedure, it also becomes restricted in its application. If faith and knowledge are to be identified, a monopoly of religion is established in favour of the intellectual man, and his attitude to the unphilosophic vulgar becomes one of lofty disdain. This consequence of an intellectualistic view of religion has been well marked both in the East and the West, wherever faith has been confused with knowledge.

This identification and restriction is fully admitted, and in many cases commended, by the composers of the Upanishads. "The highest mystery in the Vedanta, delivered in a former age, should not be given to one whose passions have not been subdued, nor to one who is not a son, or who is not a pupil."[1] The emphasis upon external conditions in the second clause is a carrying out of the idea that the Upanishads contain secret doctrines, which are to be imparted only to the few. This tendency of intellectualism finds ready acceptance in a country where the caste spirit is strong. Indeed, it might be said that the caste system is a concrete embodiment of the tendency.

There is action and reaction between the two kinds of exclusiveness—the intellectual and the social—resulting in the strengthening of both. It is allowed, indeed, that for the people of the lower and illiterate classes an inferior kind of salvation may be provided, but this is regarded often by the educated classes as salvation hardly worth having. In any case, the means towards the higher and fuller salvation are not regarded as available for the Sudra or low caste person. In various parts of the literature terrible penalties are threatened for those who venture to teach the doctrine of the Vedas to a Sudra. We are told that the "ears of the Sudra who hears the Vedas are to be filled with molten lead and lac," and, if he dares pronounce them, his tongue is to be slit. The extreme of inherent exclusiveness is revealed in the saying, "A Sudra is like a cemetery. Therefore the Veda is not to be read in the vicinity of a Sudra."

It may be argued, certainly, that in the course of history we find this attitude combined with an approbation of an idolatrous system in which the needs of the lower classes are recognised, and that therefore it is unfair to press the charge of absolute exclusiveness. But this provision and authorisation of idolatry seems rather to be an attempt to find an excuse for the intellectualistic attitude. It is by no means a transformation of it or an improvement upon it. The spirit of exclusiveness is still there. The lower classes are provided with separate spiritual food, which the intellectual man can

---

[1] Cf. *Syetasvatara Upanishad* VI, 22.

not consistently touch. Idol-worship is not something—except for social reasons—which he may share, in full sympathy with their point of view, with the uneducated. It is a provision which his philosophical attitude does not really admit of. Where all is divine, it is illegitimate to speak of a concentration of divinity. For this reason the appearance of catholicity remains an appearance only, and is certainly not a deduction—except by way of degradation—from the central philosophical position.

It is, of course, possible to argue that the exclusiveness arose from a high sense of the value of religious truth and also from a pedagogic impulse. The truth to be imparted was reckoned so precious that extreme care had to be exercised in its communication. There may be a genuine reflection of the idea "that only the pure in heart may see God," and, if this is so, criticism would not be in place.

But in order to secure an adequate defence on these lines, we should have to make sure that the *possibility* of finding purity of heart in any class of persons whatsoever was recognised, and the opportunity of manifesting it was not hedged about by artificial restrictions of birth and education. We may say much the same about the reference to the pedagogic impulse. It may be necessary to impart religious truth bit by bit, "line upon line, precept upon precept," and it may be true that only those who have mastered the lower are fit for the higher. But here, again, we must demand *equality of opportunity* before the religious ideal is satisfied. All must be granted at least the chance of passing through the necessary stages. We have, however, no assurance to this effect in the Upanishads. The matter may be put even more strongly. It may be pointed out that, even if we had this assurance, danger of exclusiveness is still lurking whenever religion is made to depend too much upon slow educational processes. Education can never rid itself entirely of certain artificial restrictions, whereas the opportunity and possibility of the highest religious friendship ought to be thrown open to man as man, and not simply as an educable man in the ordinary sense of the term. Max Müller tries to defend the exclusion of the lowest classes, by saying that "to admit them to a study of the Veda would have been like admitting naked savages to the lecture room of the Royal Institution." But this little bit of satire misses the point. It depends for its force upon the assumption that the subject matter of religion is exactly the same as that which is under investigation in the Royal Institution. If this similarity had been established, then the exclusion of the naked savages would have been natural and necessary. But what we are arguing for is that this assumption is gratuitous, and that it is nothing short of a calamity to take a view of religion which excludes from its benefits, nor merely "naked savages," but that very considerable portion of the human race who have not had the opportunity of the highest intellectual culture.

Thus we cannot satisfactorily escape from the feeling that the general tone of the Upanishads is that of a message which appeals only to the few. The vast majority of the population are left out of account. As Dr. Barnett says, "The only life worth living is that which is vouchsafed to a few elect—union of the soul with the transcendent Brahman: all other existence, whatever it may seem, is wretched—an infinite number of souls, flitting in constant sorrow and blindness through every degree of organic embodiment."[1]

What is the result of this attitude? Archer Butler points out two extreme consequences for the mass of the nation—these are "the perpetuation of ignorance and the encouragement of imposture: to both of which it manifestly tends—to the former by being unfitted for the vulgar mind and to the latter by countenancing pretences to supernatural power." Privilege is apt to produce a claim to greater privileges still. The exclusive possession of intellectual culture, when strongly emphasised and given a religious colouring, very often passes over, in the presence of masses of uneducated people filled

[1] *Brahma Knowledge*, p. 17.

with wondering admiration, into the assumption of supernatural powers. On the other hand, the ascription to the lower classes of intellectual and religious incapacity often results in a passive acknowledgement of this incapacity. This shows itself practically in the abandonment of effort and the perpetuation of ignorance.

Thus a certain amount of hopelessness is engendered amongst the excluded classes, if they are told that the only salvation possible for them is of an inferior kind, and that there is some blissful state of being from which they are shut out. Amongst the philosophers also the effect must be somewhat distressing. For the best of them, at all events, there will be a certain amount of discomfort at the thought that the salvation which is possible for them is impossible for the vast majority of their fellows. They—the privileged classes—cannot for long be content with having discovered a privilege and not a panacea. The consciousness of having no *good news* for all mankind is a somewhat chilling one, and the evangelical impulse which is characteristic of the noblest natures will not for ever consent to the denial of an outlet. If the great world has to be left in darkness, there is small consolation in the thought that a few select souls may be permitted to live in the light. It is possible that even amongst the intellectuals there may arise a dissatisfaction with their own position, and a secret admiration for that attitude of mind which is expressed in the words of St. Paul: "I am a debtor, both to the Greeks and to the Barbarians: both to the wise and to the unwise." It is certain that in such an attitude, and in such an attitude alone, lies the hope of the salvation of the world, and any philosophy which refuses to make it possible stands condemned as an unmistakeable cause of pessimism.

We must now turn to the particular metaphysical solution which is offered by the Upanishads, especially in the idealistic phase of their pantheistic teaching. It may be said, in brief, that in order to establish a satisfactory relation between the One and the Many, they have sacrificed the many to the one, and have escaped from the difficulties of the finite world by denying its reality. The problems of the finite world are regarded as no problems at all when looked at from the proper point of view, for from this point of view the world in which the problems occur may be entirely negated.

> " But what are Time and Space, whose rough intrusion
> Will separate what is so near allied?
> Are they not taught to be a mere illusion?
> May we not be against them fortified?"—*Deussen.*

Now it is no doubt a great consolation to be told that the problems which so often worry us are in reality no problems at all; but the trouble is that the deliverance which is here offered is of a temporary character, and before we know where we are, the difficulties of the actual are upon us again. We find that the method we have adopted is a little like that of the ostrich, who thinks that it has eluded all pursuit by burying its head in the sand. We find that the actual cannot be so summarily dealt with, and that if we are to establish our position we must be prepared to face some of the difficulties with which a denial of the actual world involves us. We must prove that our dream world is satisfying, and that we do not require the contributions of ordinary experience.

The teachers of the Upanishads and their followers were immediately face to face with difficulties such as these. They found themselves, *e.g.*, called upon to deal with the accusation that their philosophy resembled the sensationalism of the Buddhists, who had reduced all reality to states of consciousness having momentary existence merely. Sankara took up the defence at this point, and tried to show that external things have existence, for the simple reason that we are conscious of them. "If there is nothing external how can anything even seen to be external?"[1] It is unfair to compare waking experience to a dream, for dreams do not fit in with the rest of our experience of waking experience.[2]

[1] Cf. Sankara's Commentary II, 2-28.
[2] Cf. Commentary on Sutra III, 2-3.

The difficulty about this defence is that if the whole of waking experience ought to be regarded as a dream, it is difficult to see how it can also be called the negation of a dream. We cannot distinguish degrees of reality within a whole which is, as a whole, imaginary. In the course of an ordinary dream we may, no doubt, distinguish between imaginary occurrences and what we take, during the course of the dream, to be actual occurrences. But this distinction holds only as long as the dream lasts. When we realise that the whole is a dream, both what we held to be imaginary and what we hold to be real experiences alike fall down to the level of unrealities. Similarly, when we reach the stage of enlightenment at which we may say that life as a whole is a dream, we cannot continue to distinguish degrees of reality within that dream. Thus it would seem that notwithstanding all efforts to adjust ourselves on this point to the requirements of more ordinary thinking, we remain firmly fixed within the dilemma either of saying that our total experience is a dream, in which case no part of it can have reality, or of saying that certain parts of it have reality, in which case it cannot as a whole be a dream.

Another method of adjustment to the empirical consciousness is found in the doctrine of two orders of knowledge. Mr. Gough, *e.g.*, says, "Individual souls and their environments are true for the many. They are real from the standpoint of everyday experience. The visions of a dream are false from this standpoint. Individual souls and their environments are false for the reflective few. Their existence disappears in the higher existence—they are unreal from the standpoint of metaphysical truth."[1] Now to speak of the popular and scientific points of view is quite legitimate, provided that you can show that the latter takes account of and corrects and completes the former. But simply to leave the two views side by side is no adjustment of this kind. It is merely to say that what may be true on one level is false on another level, without assigning any reason for

[1] *Phil. of the Upanishads*, p. 197.

the change. You cannot reconcile two contradictory doctrines by saying that one class of person holds one doctrine and another class holds the other doctrine. If you do not go further than this, it is simply dogmatism to say that the empirical point of view must be entirely abandoned. We must suggest a reason for the choice between them, otherwise we shall be in the position of a man who expresses a preference for one swing of the pendulum rather than the other. Truth must be a unity, and, if there are certain aspects of experience which we cannot bring within this unity, we must either widen the unity so as to embrace them, or we must honestly deny them and take the consequence of our denial. We cannot pretend to deal with them by relegating them, when they become disconcerting, to a lower level of experience, and graciously permitting their consideration by an inferior order of minds. If we admit that these facts are worthy of consideration at all, they must be taken into consideration by the higher order of mind as well. They cannot simply be disregarded, if our philosophy is to have any claim to completeness; and yet the distinction between two orders of knowledge, such as is implied in the Upanishads, involves such disregard.

Other defenders of the idealistic phase of the Upanishad teaching would call in the aid of modern philosophical parallels. They would compare their doctrine to the idealism of Berkeley, or they would cite the phenomenalism of Kant. We are by no means committed to the opinion that, even if such comparisons were established, the position would thereby be adequately defended, but it is sufficient in the meantime to show that the comparisons are in themselves hardly legitimate.

What difference, it is asked, is there between the illusion theory of the Upanishads, and the theory of Berkeley which reduces all reality to a series of ideas in the mind of God. In reply, it may be said that Berkeley does not wield the weapon of illusion with nearly so wide a sweep. Berkeley has, indeed, discarded the doctrine of the independent reality of external things, but this certainly does not mean that they have no reality of any kind, or that the system in which they find a place is altogether an illusion. It is rather a system of signs—a language expressive, in a fixed and orderly manner, of the mind of God. It is a system in which every part has meaning in relation to the whole.

Max Müller again falls back upon comparison with the relation between the phenomenal and the noumenal in the philosophy of Kant. "The substantial reality of the world is not denied, for that rests on Brahman, but all that we see and hear by our limited senses, all that we perceive and conceive and name, is purely phenomenal, as we say—is the result of Avidya, as the Vedantists say. This does not mean that the phenomenal world is altogether nothing—no, it is always the effect of which Brahman is the cause; and, as there cannot be any substantial difference between cause and effect, the phenomenal world is ultimately as real as Brahman, nay, in its ultimate reality, is Brahman itself."[1] Thus the illusory in the Upanishads means just the same as the phenomenal in Kant. Yet, though there is a surface similarity, there seems to be a fundamental difference which Max Müller, and those who think like him, have overlooked. When Western philosophers point out that the things of ordinary experience are merely phenomenal, they do not thereby divest them altogether of meaning and attribute them to a principle of irrationality. But this is just what we do find to a very large extent in the Upanishads. The charge of unreality is pressed much further back than in what might be called the phenomenalism of much Western philosophy. The world is a gigantic product of ignorance or nescience, which can be dealt with only by negation and not by interpretation.

For this reason the thought of the Upanishads is not at liberty, as Berkeley is, to rehabilitate some of our experiences, by giving them a place in a rational system of signs, nor can it, with Kant, treat the

[1] *Lectures on the Vedanta*, p. 87.

phemonenal as leading back, even by implication to the noumenal. All the phenomenal, together with all its meaning, must be swept away into the realm of illusion, in order that ultimately a pure unity alone may remain. At least this is logically the implication of the doctrine of nescience, though these implications may not always be drawn out to their full extent.

Thus it must be admitted that the adjustments which Upanishad thinkers and their defenders attempt to make between their own idealistic doctrine and the data of ordinary experience have not been particularly successful. The reason of the failure is that the Upanishads attempt to satisfy two contradictory demands. For religious and ethical purposes, *i.e.*, in order to provide a way of deliverance and salvation, they asserted the dreamlike character of ordinary experience, but, at the same time, in order to keep up an appearance of harmony with this experience, they attempted to distinguish degrees within this dream, and permitted all except a few who possessed pre-eminent qualifications to accept certain portions of this dream as real. The dilemma they are in is a serious one. When attention is concentrated on the negative movement of the soul, a breach seems to be forced with existence as a whole, and with the way in which things happen in the world. The construction of the theory of *Maya* is the symbol of the consciousness of this breach, and if this doctrine, which, as we have seen, finds predominant support in the Upanishads, could be carried through, a way of deliverance would be provided, though perhaps at excessive cost. The distance, however, which this theory has travelled from ordinary experience, sometimes appals those who hold it, and they attempt to give some degree of reality to the facts of life. In so doing, however, they close the only way to salvation which has hitherto been pointed out. They find that experience refuses to be negated, and that in trusting to merely negative procedure they have attempted an impossible task. They have emptied life of its contents, and have given up the power of "penetration and organisation" of reality—or at least of the reality of ordinary experience. When they come back to it again—as sooner or later they must do—this ordinary reality presents itself as an unintelligible mass out of connection with the reality, which, in the course of their philosophic searching, they have been accustomed to regard as central or even exclusive. When, further, they take up the burden of the ordinary again and attempt to organise it, they find that their way of deliverance is closed. They are now so firmly caught in the toils of the world of what is called ordinary fact that it seems presumption to call it illusion.

Thus, in confusion and darkness of mind, the seeker after truth in the Upanishads stands between two worlds. If he is swayed by a desire for deliverance, he must altogether reject the data which most men would regard as real: if he still retains a respect for ordinary experience, he must give up his hope of deliverance. His philosophy, therefore, can satisfy neither the mystic who looks to it for deliverance, nor the more ordinary man who looks to it for power to penetrate experience. Dissatisfaction seems to be the only possible result of this want of clearness and consistency. We cannot live in two unconnected worlds, and yet our demand for unity is left unrealised. The solution offered by the Upanishads is beyond the majority of men, and is possible for the enlightened few only, in rare moments of ecstasy, if even then. When the most of us come down again to the level of the ordinary, we find that we have still to grope our way in a darkness which is all the greater because our eyes have been dazzled by a light which has burst abruptly upon our ordinary consciousness, and has been as abruptly withdrawn. We find that we have not been able to escape, and yet we were told that our way of salvation lay in escape. Perhaps we have been searching in the wrong direction—perhaps salvation lies not in escape, but in transformation.

Before closing our discussion of the metaphysical inadequacy of the solution offered, let us look for a moment at the barrenness of its inner content. We have found that the attempt to discover agreement with ordinary experience has been for the most part a failure, but we could reconcile ourselves more easily to this failure if we could be sure that the transcendental world for which we have sacrificed so much, is itself of a positive and satisfying character. The goal of the system is God, but who or what is the God it would reach? Our conclusion on this point is very similar to that which we reached in regard to the character of the bliss which was offered as the supreme condition of the soul. Descriptions given are wholly negative. The predicates *sat-cit-ananda* are applied to God, and we should be satisfied with them if they retained their usual meanings. But the Being is a mystical combination of Being and not being. It is a denial of Being in any empirical sense, and an assertion of it in some vague transcendental sense which removes it from the reach of human aspiration and the range of human comprehension. It is the same with the other predicates. The intellect which God is said to possess is in no way akin to ours, with all its categories and forms. He is the abstract unity of thought, and unknowable. Even the intuition wherewith he may be grasped is an inconsistency, for no individual minds are left in which the intuition may become a reality. The bliss also which is ascribed to God, and which may be ours by union with him, contains, as we have seen, none of the elements of human happiness, and can be described only by comparison with dreamless sleep. Deussen thus presents the concept in all its emptiness, "The Being of the *Atman* is no being as revealed in experience, and in an empirical sense is rather a not-being; and, similarly, the 'thought' is only the negation of all objective being, and the bliss is the negation of all suffering—as this exists in deep dreamless sleep."[1]

God is thus unattainable, and we have given up our ordinary world for the sake of a negation. It is what might have been expected, for we have denied the world

[1] Deussen, *Upanishads*, p. 404.

from which we might argue to God, and we have denied the very existence of ourselves, who might have sustained the argument. This abnormality of our procedure will be commented on a little later, but surely the thought of the result in all its unattainability and its negativity is a source of pessimism. There is very little to distinguish it, as an Indian writer says, "from the absolute nihilism of Buddha and his followers." The "Nothing" and the "All" lie, indeed, very close together. Faust says, "In thy nothing the All I hope to find," but, sometimes, the human consciousness transforms this into a fear that in the "all" only "nothing" will be discovered.

In so far as this confession of failure to attain to a knowledge of God is an indication of humility, it is wholly admirable. The spirit of the *Kena Upanishad*, *e.g.*, in its emphasis upon the point that Brahman is beyond the ordinary categories of knowledge, is one with which it is possible to have very considerable sympathy. We may agree that, if our worship of God is based upon the same kind of attitude as would be appropriate to an object of sense perception, our worship is likely to be illusory, and we may agree also with the sentiment of II, 11: "Only he who does not know it, knows it. It is not known by him who knows it, but is known by him who knows it not." We cannot demand of any philosophy that it should provide a means of knowing God by the ordinary means of knowing. As a recent writer has said, "The clear and distinct ideas by which man manipulates and organises his temporal experience are painfully insufficient when he strives to construe through them the ground of all experience, and the highest category at his disposal cannot exhaust the depth and riches of the Absolute."[1] We must admit that the knowledge of God, if it is to be gained at all, is possible only after long and diligent search, and we must recognise the need of Divine help throughout. We must admit that, in the end, even God cannot be completely known. But it is possible to make too much of the difficulty of the

[1] Galloway, *Development of Religious Experience*, p. 130.

search, to transform the unknown into the unknowable, to despair of certainty altogether, to conceive of God as altogether out of relation to human faculties—and in the Upanishads these possibilities become actualities. We may justly object to crude anthropomorphism, but our objection in this respect does not mean that God is out of relation to our personality altogether, and that human modes of conception cannot make at least some approach to an understanding of His being. There is all the difference in the world between ascribing to God a definite personality exactly similar to ours and interpreting him *through* our personality. Further, does the insufficiency, of our conceptions involve their entire unreliability. Even though we cannot attain to absolute certainty, may it not be that religious certainty is the highest kind of certainty we *can* attain to. There is much truth in Eucken's words, "We maintain that it is a very poor conception of religion which deems any certainty superior to hers, and does not claim for her truth a far more primary certainty than that of the formula $2 \times 2 = 4$."[1]

This distrust of our faculties which is manifested in the Upanishads, condemns us to intellectual hopelessness and deprives us of a divine defence in our struggle with ordinary experience in all its unintelligibility. It is thus directly productive of a pessimistic outlook upon life. We shall see more clearly how this is so, if we take account of the following considerations:—

1. This distrust involves an *abnormal* treatment of human nature and experience. The ideal which is set before us is not reached by the natural and normal working of our human faculties, or by a proper consideration of the facts of human experience. The normal tendency of the human mind is to allow existence to create a belief in the value of the continuance of that existence, and seems to be fundamentally opposed to theories which have as their main purpose not to explain existence but to show how it may most surely cease to be. It is at least a justifiable assumption that a faculty

[1] Eucken, *Christianity and the New Idealism*, p. 29.

which is in existence is meant to be used, and the normal idea would seem to be "to build into character the whole potentiality of our nature." We have been given certain tools, and it would be foolish not to use them, especially if, sometimes at least, they make sense and give satisfaction. The teaching of the Upanishads, however, would sometimes seem to imply that our faculties are given to us that we may destroy them. If we were to follow this teaching, we should find ourselves out of touch with the universe we live in, and sooner or later there would arise in us the feeling that the "world is out of joint." And we fail to reach even the ideal of holiness which is supposed to tempt us to renunciation, for, as has been said, "If there is any way by which a man can baulk the realisation of moral excellence it is by a studied repression of all that he has in him to become." Again, it seems abnormal not to take account of the whole of experience. It is a contradiction of our faith in existence. Until we have clear proof to the contrary, we may assume that all the facts of existence are worth taking account of. The *onus probandi* is always on those who negate. We may conclude our consideration of this point by quoting the opinion of two of the leading philosophical writers of our time. Sir Henry Jones says: "I should say that *prima facie* it is a grave argument against a philosophy that it contradicts the principles which the world has found valuable in practice. In one respect, at least, common sense is truer than any philosophy and serves as its criterion. And it is a positive achievement for a philosopher to be orthodox, provided his orthodoxy is philosophic. He comes neither to invent nor to destroy, but to fulfil; he rises above the fundamental convictions of mankind not by rejecting but by comprehending them."[1] Again, Bradley says, "If metaphysic is to stand, it must, I think, take account of all sides of our being. I do not mean that every one of our desires must be met by a promise of particular satisfaction, for that would be absurd and utterly impossible. But if the main

[1] Jones, *Lotze*, p. 12.

tendencies of our nature do not reach consummation in the Absolute, we cannot believe that we have attained to perfection and truth."[1]

2. The procedure of thought in the Upanishads is of an *abstract* character and this probably explains why it cannot carry the remedy for its inadequacy within itself, and by natural expansion meet some of the needs of human nature, which, in its first form, it altogether ignores. The procedure is dominated by the idea that all determination is negation. One by one you throw away the determinate qualities, as Peer Gynt, in the play of that name, peeled off the coats of the onion, until you arrive at the centre of all and find that that centre is dangerously like nothing. In logic such procedure would be called the pursuit of the abstract universal. We should notice that the process is dominated throughout by a contempt for the intermediate stages. There is no effort to show that these find a place in a more comprehensive idea. They must simply be left behind as *untruths*. They, the particulars, have not importance in themselves, nor are they trustees for the whole. Negation is triumphant; the content and structure of the world is dissolved; the ideal is absorption. Put logically, the underlying conception is that we reach the infinite by denying the finite, which practically involves the somewhat gloomy assumption that "merely not to be in the finite world is logically and *per se* a presumable gain."[2] From a slightly different point of view we may be said to reconcile ourselves with the universe by reducing both ourselves and the universe to nothingness. It is doubtful, however, whether two emptinesses can supply anything worthy of being called a reconciliation.

What chiefly concerns us here is that this abstract procedure involves ultimately a degradation of the intellect, a deadening down of its peculiar powers. Thus, in order to solve its problems it has to go beyond itself as psychical, and have recourse to conceptions which belong

---

[1] *Appearance and Reality*, p. 148.

[2] Bosanquet, *Value and Destiny of the Individual*, p. 255.

rather to the realm of biology and even of physics. There is much truth in Bergson's contention, that pure and empty unity is met with only in space, is that of a mathematical point, and that what is psychical cannot be crushed into spatial forms. Yet we disregard this caution, and, led on by our love of abstraction and helped by spatial metaphors, we conceive of the world as a vast space which can gradually be emptied of objects. When we attempt to put our thought alongside this emptiness, we reach the same vacuity of thought. Crozier describes this abdication of the intellect in a somewhat different way. According to him the abstract procedure leads to the Vital Principle being substituted for the Intellect as the First Cause of things. We come dangerously near a conception of what is merely "universal life," and regard salvation as consisting in what is little more than physical participation. As Crozier puts it, "The vital principle, the *Anima Mundi*, which is the life of Nature, is the supreme principle to which all else pays homage,—the Intellect being regarded as but an evanescent foam-bubble thrown up to the surface of its deep and ever-flowing stream."[1] We do not mean to suggest that this sacrifice of the intellect is always conscious, but it may be none the less actual. Thought by constant negation negates even itself, and loses itself in empty immensity or is absorbed in a central physical life, a merely physical life.

3. Our last consideration in this chapter is, that if abstract thought leads to emptiness, the human soul will not be content with this emptiness, but will seek to satisfy itself *by way of reaction*. It will give itself up to emotionalism, it will lay emphasis upon the lower impulses of human nature and will satisfy its religious needs by a capricious polytheism.

The emptiness of the religious ideal, when we try to realise what it means, at once reveals its connection with lower forms of experience, sometimes with the merely physical, and sometimes with the merely

[1] *Intellectual Development*, p. 5.

emotional. Thus the way is prepared for the cults, which play so large a part in Indian religions. Sometimes the reaction takes a beautiful and poetical form, such as that described in the following passage from a renowned Brahmo leader: "The warm love of Hari glowed in the heart of Narada as that saintly rishi, white with age, sang and played on his vina. The boy, Prahlada, a king's son and destined to fill the throne, shed many tears over Hari's beloved name, and suffered persecution, the recital of which in popular ballads still makes many eyes wet. It is said that Vyasa, after he had written the great poem of the *Mahabharata*, felt restless in his mind, and, with the object of obtaining the peace he so much needed, spoke with Narada, 'Thou has written of wisdom, Narada, and of the merit of works, thou hast taught men of the things of the world. This cannot give me joy and peace.' 'Speak, Oh Vyasa, of the love of God, and thy heart will be at rest.' This great bard accordingly discoursed of the sweetness of bhakti, and his spirit departed in gladness and tranquillity to the mansions of the blessed."[1]

Frequently, however, the reaction follows the lines of the degradation of the intellect which we have already hinted at. The house of the soul is swept and garnished and undesirable guests enter in and make their home there—phantasies and extravagances, arbitrary and unrestrained in their construction. Seeing that the higher activities have failed to produce a comforting result, recourse is had to the lower. Even in minds of higher culture, scepticism may give place to extravagant theory under the influence of the idea that where no real knowledge is possible any wild imagination may take its place, and the intellect having abdicated its position, feeling becomes unrestrained. The uncontrolled imagination, inspired by unrestrained feeling, proceeds to invent objects of worship in a purely arbitrary fashion, and is apt to borrow materials for the representation of the divine from carnal rather than from spiritual experi-

[1] *Brahma Samaj*, p. 31 (Mazumdar).

ences. Here we have the explanation of the confused welter of polytheism in Indian religion, with the attendant belief in magic and in material sacrifice. At first sight this seems utterly repugnant to the pure intellectualism of the philosophical system, but it is easily understood when it is viewed as a reaction from an intellectualism which has revealed the poverty of its results. Polytheism is a case of rushing to an opposite extreme. When the phenomenal turns out to be altogether illusory, it does not much matter what we do with it. Practically the swing of the pendulum is from asceticism to indulgence, theoretically it is from a disdainful idealism to a facile naturalism. We may pass—sometimes by way of materialism and sometimes more directly—to revel in the particular and multiply gods for the satisfaction of every wandering imagination and every impulse of the senses. We may become sentimentalists in religion without let or hindrance. In one of his novels, Meredith says, "When a wise man makes a false step, will he not go further than a fool?" The false step here has been that of abstract procedure, which has resulted in dissatisfaction. This dissatisfaction, again, has attempted to cure itself by a descent in the scale of worth, by a substitution of imagination for reason, by physical enjoyment for intellectual blessedness.

But, again, we realise that the satisfaction which is the result of exercise of the lower faculties, rather than of the higher, or which is dependent on mere feeling, cannot be permanent. The higher minds in India cannot and do not find satisfaction in the confusion of polytheism and the disregard of their higher spiritual nature. Those who have turned from the weariness of scepticism to imaginary mythologies will soon find scepticism attacking their unstable constructions. Even the common people will find that the advance of thought and civilisation have taken away their gods. And the lesson is simply this—that we must revise the procedure which has thus ended in pessimism and gloom or at the best has provided an insufficient remedy. The intellect cannot permanently abdicate her rights, but neither can she supply a remedy by repeating her negative procedure or insisting upon her exclusive privileges. The remedy lies rather in discovering higher functions of the intellect than those of mere abstraction, and relating it, with an exceeding closeness of relation, to the other powers of a complete human nature.

But before we say more about the remedy, we must point out one or two other effects of the main tendency of the philosophy we have under consideration.

CHAPTER V

The Religious and Ethical Effects

WE have spoken of the intellectualism and of the metaphysical inadequacy of the teaching of the Vedanta ; we have now to inquire into the nature of the religious relationship which it establishes, and the effect of this relationship upon a general view of life. This topic is, perhaps, not one that admits of separate treatment. On the one hand, we can hardly distinguish the religious effect from the intellectual effect, for religion and philosophy are bound so closely together in all Indian thought. Even if, by reason of this identification, certain aspects may escape treatment, these aspects may be better dealt with under the heading of the ethical and the practical. Yet, in thus disclaiming the necessity of any detailed examination of the religious effect, we are not to be understood as suggesting that the teaching of the Upanishads was not intended to be religious. We are simply pointing out that the religious aspect is so intimately bound up with other aspects as to be incapable of separate treatment. There are some, indeed, who argue that this system was never intended to be religious. Worsley, *e.g.*, holds that it is a mistake to expect it to support religious values. He accepts, without surprise, the fact that the Indian philosophic religion has made but few converts outside the class of those who originally held it, and he indicates that the reason of this is, that its teachers regarded it as really a philosophy, and " philosophy is not for the bulk of humanity, but for the chosen few." Moreover, "Hindu philosophy demands such abstruse and subtle phases of thought that the number of persons able to follow the doctrines and thoroughly grasp them must always remain limited."[1] We may have discovered, and we

[1] *Concepts of Monism*, p. 168.

may still further discover, that the secret of the inadequacy of the religious effect lies just in this identification of the religious and the philosophical points of view, but this resulting weakness is quite a different matter, and does not alter the fact of the identification in the minds of the upholders of the system, or enable us to say that they did not intend to produce a religious effect. We may come to the conclusion that the attempt to do the work of a religion by means of a philosophy is an illegitimate one, but this does not detract from the religious character of the aim. The effort to win release from the *Samsara* and to attain to union with the Divine is the product of an essentially religious impulse, and Max Müller was right in holding that what distinguishes the teaching of the Upanishads from all other philosophies is that "it is at the same time a religion and a philosophy."

Nevertheless, we may notice that the provision for other than philosophical satisfaction of the religious impulse is extremely meagre, and we may examine some of the dangers which result from the merging of the religious in the philosophical point of view, and especially from laying the chief emphasis on the purely or predominantly intellectual relation of identity.

The conception of identity is a beautiful one, and at first sight seems to supply us with an ideal of communion. There are certain moods of mind when absorption presents itself as a desirable consummation. Mysticism, which is largely based on this idea, has been called religion in its intensest form, and is, by universal consent, an important element in every religion. Indeed, the conception of identity might be said to be an attempt to represent metaphysically the emotional glow of religious satisfaction, which should attend every successful effort towards communion with the Divine. At the same time, this form of representation is misleading if, as it seems to do, it suggests that this satisfaction is permanent. As we all know, emotional satisfaction is subject to incessant variation, and the intellectual relation under which we symbolise it, ought, at least, to hint at this liability to variation. Now, things which are identical with each other cannot change in their relations to each other. For this reason we would argue that identity cannot be a proper statement of the religious relationship, even when the utmost ideal of communion has been reached. Still less adequate is this statement of the religious relation for the purposes of indicating the conditions of the attainment of the religious ideal. Its vagueness makes it applicable at *any* stage of religious development, and so it is properly applicable nowhere in any effective sense. More definitely we may say that it simply leaves out of account the fundamental conditions of religious communion, those conditions which explain both its initiation and its variations. It cannot be too strongly insisted upon, that the religious relationship must be one in which two terms persist and the unity which is aimed at must be a unity including difference, and not a bare unity. If we cling to the idea of bare unity, two results are possible. Either our conception will be of an all-absorbing activity on the part of God and passivity on the part of man, or God will be merely an aspect of our own subjectivity. But if the religious relationship is to be a real one, it must subsist between two at least partially independent and distinguishable entities—between the human spirit, on the one hand, and some power distinct from, though not alien to, the human spirit, on the other hand—a relation which finds its expression in worship and corresponds to the etymology of the word communion.

We cannot give up the doubleness of the relationship. We cannot say that it is impossible to know God unless we become identified with the Object of our knowledge, or that it is impossible to love Him unless we become absorbed in his Being, or to serve Him unless we annihilate our own personality. As Leibnitz said, "Man is not a part but a counterpart of Godhead," or, as a more modern writer has put it, "That a man may love God, it is necessary that there should be not only a God to be loved but a man to love Him."[1] Worship is impossible on the basis of identity.

We are in these days becoming more and more dissatisfied with the idea of an all-absorbing unity in religion or in knowledge. Some would say that it is because we are becoming more irreligious, that we find the idea of an overwhelming Divine Reality distasteful to us. The explanation may, however, lie in another direction. Our dissatisfaction with the idea of a pure idealistic or pantheistic unity may arise from the fact that this idea is false to the method by which we normally construct our knowledge, and, therefore, is not a conception of God which we may legitimately entertain, if we are to give due consideration to the requirements of human nature. We are coming to see that in the construction of experience in general the *activity* of the individual must be given a more important place. In religious experience, in particular, also, full weight must be given to this activity. We see clearly that the religious consciousness includes, as one of its essential constituents, a feeling of effort or straining towards the ideal. So we cannot accept any idea of pantheistic identity which would weaken the validity of this feeling. If the idea of one sole agent is emphasised, we may ask how the individual soul has power even to initiate its return to God. Nay, we may go further, and ask how such a separation from God ever arose as may explain the religious yearning after return. If we are already what we wish to be, the wish for return to God becomes superfluous. Why should we desire to become the sons of God, if we already *are* the sons of God. If it is replied that we are the sons of God but not yet in the fullest sense, seeing that we have identified ourselves with the finite things of the world and not with the universal subject, we may ask, whence comes this false identification? And who may make it if there is only the one reality? The truth is that if the principles of the Upanishads were to be carried out to their logical conclusions, all possibility of explaining the rise of the

[1] Chesterton, *Orthodoxy*, p. 243.

religious consciousness would be taken away. If it were not a contradiction in terms, we might say that the religious consciousness would have remained unconscious, inarticulate. And the same holds good, as we have already hinted, in regard to the consummation of the religious relationship. We cannot attain to fulness of communion, unless we retain our consciousness both of ourselves and of God. "A mind cannot have communion with itself or with part of itself."[1]

If we look upon the relation of identity more from the side of the subject, as the Upanishads teach us continually to do, the obstacles to a proper religious relationship seem equally insurmountable. We hear much in the Upanishads of the universal subject. By retiring within our consciousness, and getting deeper than consciousness, we discover the identity between the individual Atman and Brahman. In this case the subjective seems to absorb the objective, and the shut eyes of the mediæval mystic are typical. But, as Dr. E. Caird says, in another connection, "A God who is within and not without is no God at all." With the loss of the object comes also the loss of that subjective life for which the sacrifice is made. For the subject has no meaning except in relation to the objective world, ... and its freedom from that world would turn into its own extinction."[2] The application may be made to the philosophy of the Upanishads. If God cannot be made in any sense an object, he disappears into the mists of abstraction. In any case he cannot be worshipped, and we lose the "life" of religious devotion. In the religious life we cannot afford to lose sight altogether of the conception of a power not ourselves—we must go out beyond ourselves.

And in thus going beyond ourselves in the religious consciousness, we shall see more clearly the unsatisfactoriness of the purely abstract conception of God, which was all that the metaphysic of the Upanishads could offer us. We can find the consolation and the

---

[1] Rashdall, *Philosophy of Religion*, p. 102.

[2] *Evolution of Religion*, I, p. 381.

strength which we need only in a spirit like our own. We can perfect our powers of intelligence and of love, only by contact with an Infinite who is also intelligence and love.

After all, it is impossible that our faith in God should be altogether different from our faith in man. We have seen that it is abnormal to prefer the lower to the higher, and this abnormality we are guilty of if we say that faith in the impersonal is higher than faith in the personal. If we conceive of God as other than personal, the probabilities are that we shall soon come to conceive of him as something lower than personal—as substance or as force. But entrance into the religious relationship ought surely rather to mean a heightening and completion of our ideas of the best human relationships.

The necessity of an advance along the lines of personality is felt within the limits of Hindu thought. The *nirguna* aspect of Brahman gives place to the *saguna* aspect, and it is argued that the later aspect may be kept in view for all practical purposes of worship. Dr. Thibaut points out the felt inadequacy of the purely negative aspect. "The only forms of the Vedantic philosophy which can at any time have been popular, are those in which the Brahman of the Upanishads has somehow transformed itself into a being between whom and the devotee there can exist a personal relation—love and faith on the part of man, justice tempered by mercy on the part of the divinity. The only books of widespread influence are such as the *Ramayana* of Tulsidas, which lay no stress on the distinction between an absolute Brahman, inaccessible to all human wants and sympathies and a shadowy Lord whose very conception depends on the shadowy principle of Maya; but love to dwell on the delight of devotion to one all-wise and merciful ruler, who is willing to lend a gracious ear to the supplication of the worshipper."[1]

Dr. Thibaut has probably in mind a quotation such as the following, from Tulsidas: "The saint gave

---

[1] Introduction to Sankara's Commentary, p. 128.

me the fullest possible instruction, but the worship of the impersonal laid no hold upon my heart. Again I cried, bowing my head at his feet, 'Tell me, holy Father, how to worship the incarnate. . . . . When I have seen my fill of the Lord, then I will listen to your sermon on the unembodied.' Again, the saint discoursed of the incomparable Hari; and, demolishing the theory of the incarnation, expounded him as altogether passionless. But I rejected the theory of the abstract, and with much obstinacy insisted upon his concrete manifestation, the religion of the impersonal did not satisfy me. I felt an overpowering devotion toward an incarnation of the Supreme."[1]

Thus we find, even within Hinduism itself, a revolt against a religion of the impersonal and a yearning after a personal Redeemer. The principle of identity, which is the fundamental principle of the Upanishads, has been left behind, and satisfaction has been sought for in a more concrete and objective conception of the Divine. The religion of the impersonal has failed to satisfy, and yet the Upanishads have not provided a satisfactory basis for a fuller relationship. In this failure lies one of the reasons for its pessimistic tendency. It is not sufficient, as Max Müller seems to think (Cf. *Lectures on the Vedanta*, p. 84), to provide a God who will be sufficient for *practical purposes*. Religion demands an absolute, and will not be content with the "qualified" God if the "unqualified" is the ultimate truth and the only ultimate truth. Yet, if in order to reach the absolute the enlightened man has to leave behind him all belief in the qualified Brahman, we may ask whether what he has thrown away is not more valuable than what he has retained.

Further, esoteric procedure in religion is ultimately impossible. The enlightened man cannot keep his beliefs to himself, they will filter down to the less enlightened, and these also will be dissatisfied with a God who exists only for practical purposes. If, on the other hand, the highest wisdom leaves to us only a vague

---

[1] *Ramayana of Tulsidas.*

communion with, or participation in, a Being who is little better than a negation, our own souls partake of the emptiness of this negation. In any case, we are left helpless in the sweep of forces which—empirical though they may be—still continue to exert their influence upon us. We have failed to find a true religious deliverance, and are bound once more in fetters from which we have no power to shake ourselves free. We cannot be content in the religious relationship with negation and passivity, and yet this is all the Upanishads seem to afford us when we keep most strictly to the main lines of their teaching. As Eucken puts it, "These utterances of Hindu conviction affect us by their simplicity and sincerity, but they set the whole theme of life in a lower key, and they deprive it of all strong stimulus."[1]

We may now turn to the more purely ethical consequences of the teaching of the Upanishads, and ask whether it is a reinforcement of life in the moral struggle. Does it enable us to make a truly ethical distinction between good and evil? Does it secure the permanence of the good and encourage us with the belief that we may effectively strive for the attainment of it? Is the universe capable of progress, and is the good character which we may win in the process of contributing to his progress to be regarded as a lasting possession of the individual soul? Or, do all these distinctions, permanent valuations, and hopes belong to an unreal world which we should treat ultimately with indifference?

It is often alleged that the teaching we are considering involves the transcendence of moral distinctions, and we must first of all discuss this point. Now, seeing that, as we have frequently had occasion to observe, the strength of the system lies rather in what it denies than in what it affirms, and this denial includes the denial of evil and of all chance and wandering desires, surely we may here expect an ethical system of the utmost purity. Mystical absorption will lead to detachment

---

[1] *Christianity and the New Idealism*, p. 75.

from the very region of temptation. This spirit of freedom from evil would seem to be discoverable in *Chhandogya Upanishad* IV, 14, 3: "As water does not cling to a lotus, so no evil deed clings to him who knows it." There is a severe condemnation of evil deeds in the the same Upanishad, V, 10, 9. Also in the *Isa Upanishad* V, 12, we have the expression of a simple yearning for moral purity. "Keep us free from crooked evil, and we shall offer thee praise." Further, the stages in the ascetic life seem to imply a growing self-renunciation and a more intense appreciation of the demands of a higher life. The penetration of the various sheaths must imply an increasing freedom from the illusions of human life in which so frequently the strength of temptation lies. In short, an ideal of detachments seems to be presented, and a loosening of the ties which bind us to the earth is the result aimed at. "We shall go about our own work," in Newman's words, "as soldiers go to battle, without a care for the consequences."

Still, there are certain other considerations which move us to ask whether this quotation does represent fully the ideal set before us in the *Upanishads*. By being "without a care for the consequences," we may assume that Newman means carelessness as to personal risks, danger or pain, and we may freely admit that the Upanishads do encourage such oblivion. But there are other consequences in regard to which we cannot be so careless if we wish to preserve our energy of action. Speaking more generally, can we go about our work with full energy if we have no due sense of the value of work, and if, further, we cannot have any confidence that this work will lead to any valuable end, such as the victory of our cause, or, in the ethical life, the permanent triumph of the good? It is not sufficient to transcend the evil if we must also transcend the good.

In the Upanishads we have found that the position of works is on the whole a subordinate one, and they are intended to be merely preparatory to a life of contemplation. Thus it becomes difficult to lay sufficient emphasis upon the distinctions of the moral life, which is pre-eminently a life of action. And, as a matter of fact, we find several passages in the Upanishads which teach the transcendence of both good and evil. The absorption at which we aim sweeps within the range of its negation both good and evil deeds, and the enlightened man need no longer have regard to moral rules. The *Brihadaranyaka Upanishad* tells us that the "self becomes no greater by good works, no less by evil works." There is similar teaching in the *Taittiriya Upanishad* II, 9: "The thought afflicts not him; what have I left undone, what evil done"; and also in the *Kaushitaki Upanishad* I, 4, where we read that "when the enlightened man comes to the river Vijara he there shakes off his good and evil deeds." The third section of the same Upanishad is even more emphatic: "He who knows me," says Indra, in this section, "by no deed of his is his life harmed, not by the murder of his mother, not by the murder of his father, not by theft, not by the killing of a Brahman. If he is going to commit sin, the bloom does not depart from his face."

The consideration of such passages as these, especially the last, might seem to indicate that the Upanishads teach freedom from good in the sense of a direct encouragement to license. Ram Chandra Bose, *e.g.*, speaks of the "number of wicked hearts which have been composed to sleep by the opiate of its false hopes."[1] This, however, is an extreme conclusion based too much upon isolated passages. On the other hand, it does seem necessary to criticise the system on the ground that it does not guard sufficiently against the morally disastrous consequences which may be deduced from the doctrine of the transcendence of *both* good and evil. Most of the defenders of the system have successfully refuted the charge of direct incitement to evil, but they have not been equally successful in refuting the charge of insufficient protection of the good. They have rightly condemned the desire to acquire merit by means of particular good acts, but they have not sufficiently realised the ethical value of the

[1] Cf. *Hindu Philosophy*, p. 359

general desire for the permanence of the good. They are justified in their contention that the enlightened man will not do evil, but is he provided with a sufficient reason for the doing of good? Is it not a matter of indifference whether he continues to act at all? May he not "live as it happens"?

There is a frequent tendency amongst the supporters of the Upanishad doctrine to look upon the highest religious state as one in which morality is left behind. *Bhakti*, *e.g.*, is a further stage which we reach *after* we have fully performed the duties of the moral life. It is an "extra" to the moral life, and not the consummation of it or the spring of it. Morality is lowered to the position of a spiritual gymnastic. It is not essentially connected with the highest religious position. The enlightened man looks down from a superior height upon morality, as upon a stage which he has transcended. He himself may most assuredly continue to respect all the requirements of morality, but he does not seem to give to morality all the support of his exalted position. Is there not often a slight suggestion that morality is a problem for souls of lower rank? Is there not also a danger that these souls of lower rank may think too soon that they themselves have reached the higher level, and may abandon the sphere of morality before they have performed all its duties? The point of view which may be no danger to the enlightened man is certainly a danger to them. The thought of the goal which is to be reached ought never to be of such a character as to diminish our attention to the means which are necessary to reach it. The relation of the highest ideal—call it ethical or call it religious—to the moral life is always, in Green's words, "A further stage of the same journey."

But, in order that they may deny the evil of the world, and also in order that they may dissociate themselves from all particular action with a view to reward, the teachers of the Upanishads refuse to carry moral distinctions with them to the highest life, or to use them for the purposes of describing the ultimate unity. Evil is only ignorance. With enlightenment it will disappear, for then we shall understand that both good and evil alike belong to the unreal world, the world of semblances. Good as well as evil has been thought out of existence. The metaphysical justification for this doctrine, that the ultimately real is non-ethical, seems to rest upon the argument that the good is associated with what is desired. As, however, desire involves incompleteness, the predicate good cannot be applied to anything which is by supposition complete. "We do not value the universe," it is said, "we value all else by it." But this does not mean that the universe has no value. The reason why we do not value the universe may be that it is the standard of all values. We value all other things by the nearness of their approach to the character of the whole. If the whole had no character, all valuation, even of the parts, would be impossible. A thing does not borrow its value from the fact that we or others desire it—on the contrary we desire it because it is good, or in other words because it seems to have an inalienable right to a place in a scheme of reality of a definite character. Good does not partake of the impermanence of our desires, or pass out of existence with them. The connection of good with desire does not in the least disqualify it for being a predicate of ultimate reality. It does not depend on desire. Rather we should say that the fact of desire itself, and the tendency to valuation which is implicit in all desire, would be impossible if there were not some ultimate standard of value based on the character of reality. "The ultimate identity of value and existence is the great venture of faith." It is true, of course, that in our thoughts of ultimate Reality we must discard many erroneous and limited moral predicates, but there does not seem to be sufficient metaphysical justification for thinking that we must abandon all moral predicates whatsoever. No moral predicate of any kind would be possible if we did not stand in some morally definable relation to the whole, and we cannot be definitely related to a nonentity or a pure abstraction.

We may, then, attribute goodness to the Supreme, always remembering that this does not mean that goodness in our own lives will come about as a matter of course or without our active co-operation.

It is a futile endeavour to think evil out of existence if good has to be thought out of existence as well. Evil cannot be simply negated, it must be conquered. Both theoretically and practically, good must be retained if evil is to be destroyed. We need not follow Vedantic writers in their attempts to make the doctrine of the Upanishads appear theoretically reasonable. The difficulties in which they find themselves simply illustrate the contention that they have attempted the impossible. We are more nearly concerned here with the practical consequences of this sublimation of good and evil, and these consequences are depressing. We cannot maintain this attitude of exaltation above all difference, and when we fall below it, and allow the finite to regain its power of attraction, it is evil which first tightens its grasp upon us. By our philosophy we have detached reality from the world in which we live, and consequently our life in this world is unrestrained and erratic. We are determined to action by the concrete and particular character of our experience, and can see no principle of unification or of guidance. Our conduct is determined by the circumference of our experience, rather than by the centralising ideas. We are at the mercy of every wayward impulse, and we have provided no way of escape from the confusion which thus results. We have nothing to put over against the evil forces. In our struggle against them the idea of the unreality of evil is not powerful enough. We require something more positive, and we can find such a counteractive only in the assertion of, and the belief in, the ultimate reality of goodness. Without such a faith it would seem that human nature must despairingly acquiesce in the practical dominance of evil. The metaphysical position may demand that we take up exactly the same negative attitude to evil as to good, but in practice we may not be able to maintain this neutrality, for evil is the goal which we reach along the line of least resistance.

When in distress at the moral chaos which thus results we attempt to deliver ourselves from it, the question which we immediately ask and which no amount of philosophical reasoning can prevent our asking is whether the struggle is worth while. We do not necessarily ask this question under the influence of a low and materialistic desire for reward. We need not even put the question in a personal form, especially if by personal we mean to hint at an attitude of selfishness, but we cannot entirely get away from the idea of the completion of our personal efficiency, from the idea of *finding ourselves* in an eternal reality of which goodness is an essential characteristic. This need of a warmer and more personal ideal is hinted at in the Upanishads themselves, Cf. Chhandogya VIII, 3, 2, "We reach the wishes which we have never had fulfilled and rejoin those whom we have lost if we descend into our heart where Brahman dwells. There are all our true desires, but hidden by what is false." Yet this idea of Brahman as the home of our true desires, as the reality of our projected efficiency, is not maintained, or, at least, even if our true desires are to find their satisfaction in Brahman, they are permitted to do so only by giving up all definiteness of content and losing themselves in an ocean of nothingness.

If we have the dismal consciousness that one lot happeneth to all, that there is no fully real distinction between good and evil, and that good is no more akin to the ultimate meaning of the world than evil, we cannot long continue to strive. We shall be apt to make use prematurely of the abolition of the distinction between good and evil, and ourselves act as we please. Or, if our desires are not positive and active, we shall submit too readily to the dominance of evil in the world in which we live. But such submission will be a practical judgment of pessimism. We shall go listlessly about the business of our life. Nothing is really worth striving for—not even the highest goodness—therefore why should we strive? Our efforts count for nothing in particular—therefore let them cease. We are going nowhere in particular in the journey of the soul, therefore we may go anywhere. Metaphysical emptiness and moral indifference are not far away from one another. As a modern novelist puts it, "There must be some colour of reality about the ideal, some red lamp burning before an altar to light up that utter darkness into which the mind inevitably falls, blindly and stumblingly, without such actual guiding flame as this."[1] But here we can get no support from consideration of the Ultimate Being. There is no passage from our religion and its ideal to the duties of our life, and consequently there is great danger that these may remain undone and that we fail to take our share in reducing the depressing moral confusion, which, if left to itself, must sooner or later overwhelm us, notwithstanding all the consolations of an abstract philosophy. Thus, in the end, as Eucken puts it, "there remains a cleavage between the height of the inner life and the rest of existence. There are only particular moments when the thought of the all takes complete possession of us." And we may add that, if, in these moments, the thought of the All is without moral colouring, we receive no strength for going forth to our world again; but in weakness and without protection we have once more to confront the sorrow and the pain and the evil which after all *are* there, and will continue until we take mightier weapons than abstract thinking and vague devotion wherewith to fight against them.

The next question which arises in this connection is—Granted the need of inspiration in the moral struggle, have we any power to respond to this inspiration? Have we any freedom in a real sense of the term? Are the Upanishads deterministic? The aspect of their teaching in which a certain amount of reality is allowed to the empirical world, may come up first of all for consideration, and we find that in this connection

[1] E. Temple Thurston, *City of Beautiful Nonsense*.

the standpoint of the Upanishads is one of rigid determinism. Man is simply a part of the universe and has no proper individuality nor power of initiative. He is rigidly fixed in a system, and his actions are determined not only by the past actions of the life he is now living, but also by the past actions of a whole series of lives. The knowledge of this bondage has a paralysing effect. The world-process appears as a dark fate, and is the cause not only of mental depression but of practical inactivity. We cannot be thoroughly in earnest unless we can feel that we are free to accomplish something, and, if we are simply *parts* of one system, we can have no freedom in reference to that system as a whole, and if, further, our aim is absorption in the whole, freedom of initiative will appear as altogether unimportant. There is a suggestion of fatalism in the *Kaushitaki Up*. II, 8. The forces of the universe are represented as gathered up into a dominating, predestinating power. " He makes him whom he wishes to lead up from these worlds do a good deed; and the same makes him whom he wishes to lead down from these worlds do a bad deed. And he is the guardian of the world, he is the king of the world, and he is myself."

The reference to the Self—at once individual and universal—in this quotation, suggests a method of defence against the charge of determinism. It is pointed out that transcendental freedom may be possible even though empirical freedom is impossible. After all, we are told, the self which dominates us is not an alien self. It is our own self. We are not crushed by the totality of the universal, but we ourselves are the universal, and if we can attain to the universal point of view we shall discover our freedom. The way of life prescribed is itself emancipation. We may add to the passage already quoted the following passage from the *Chhandogya* VIII, 6: "Therefore who depart from him without having discovered the self and the true desires, in all worlds there will be for them a life of unfreedom. But those who depart from here, having discovered the soul and true desires, for them there is in all worlds a life of freedom." The doctrine of determinism, it would seem, must be supplemented by a doctrine of freedom. What does it matter though we are but links in the chain of cause and effect, if the whole chain is an illusory one ? Why should we worry about the strength of the walls of the prison house if it is possible for us to get outside ?

But it is just here that the difficulty lies—How are we to get outside ? The promise of freedom is of little use to us if the power of making our escape is taken away from us. There is small comfort in telling a prisoner that there is freedom outside his prison. Yet the philosophy we are considering treats us somewhat after this fashion. It dazzles us with the prospect of freedom and at the same time emphasises our bondage. Whenever we ascribe so much reality to our experience as is necessarily involved in making it an object of thought at all, we are confronted with the doctrine of emanation and with the theory of the whole world proceeding from God and returning to Him, inevitably, remorselessly. The determinism is operative not only amidst the details of the world, but describes the connection between these details as a whole and the ultimate unity from which they emerge. Thus, if we can think of ourselves at all, we must think of ourselves as joined by necessary links with this ultimate Unity. We lose all sense of reliance upon our own individuality, all sense of responsibility. It is a mistake to think that we have done certain things. We have neither done them nor have we the power to do them. This impotence of ours affects, also, along with other aspects of our activity, the initiation of the progress towards the divine, and freedom therefore becomes an idle dream. Here, then, we have an offering of freedom with the one hand and a taking of it away with the other, and the contrast between the transcendental ideal on the one hand and the actual state of things on the other, which actual state is remorselessly described from an empirical point of view, is bound to have a depressing effect. The door of our prison house has been opened a little way, and we catch a glimpse of the country beyond. But at the same time we realise that with the devices at our disposal we can never reach this open country. We then become uncomfortable and suspicious of our visions, and, like Descartes' captive, "who, perchance, was enjoying in his dreams an imaginary liberty and begins to suspect that it is but a vision," we also "dread awaking and conspire with the agreeable illusion in order that the deception may be prolonged" (Med. 1). Only, when confronted with the facts of life we find it impossible to prolong the deception. The open door of the vision becomes the shut door of reality, and we sit in the darkness again, feeling the weight of our fetters, and realising sorrowfully that the prison-house and the fetters are real, and the open country and the freedom are illusory—so far as we are concerned.

We may ask the further question whether this freedom, even if it were possible, would be worth having. It would undoubtedly involve a diminution of many of the ills of life, and to a certain extent would be a spiritual deliverance from temptation. But the deliverance itself is not very satisfying. It is rather absorption than true freedom, and the highest virtue associated with it is resignation. It is a freedom which is gained by the sacrifice of personality rather than by the development of it. Long ago Ramanuja realised that such a freedom would bring little but disappointment. He tells us in his commentary on the *Vedanta Sutras* I, 1-1, that no pupils would remain with a teacher holding such a doctrine of the sacrifice of personality. The only freedom which is worth having must be based on the maintenance of personality. It cannot be said that the Upanishads have fulfilled this fundamental condition. They have confused the maintenance of personality with selfishness or self-will, and have adopted too readily the idea that personality is a "blunder of existence." Consequently, they have failed to grasp the true meaning of freedom, for the only freedom which is worth having is that which gives us the power to express ourselves, the right to act, and not merely to abstain from acting. We must be convinced that our souls are valuable before we can lay effective claim to the opportunity of developing them, before, *i.e.*, we can formulate a conception of freedom which will invigorate our faculties rather than benumb them, which will strengthen us to bear the burden rather than to lay it down, to accept the trust rather than to escape from it. Abstraction from an empirical life is not necessarily concentration upon spirituality. We may be delivered from the raging sea of passionate desires, but this is of little use if we perish with hunger upon a desert shore. We do not attain to the truly religious life merely by caring little for the things that are temporal, we must also care much for the things that are eternal, and chief amongst the things that are eternal are our own souls in all their infinite value. This attitude is very far from being necessarily selfish. It is rather the primary source of an energy which may be directed to the service of God and of our fellow-men.

The mention of energy of action leads us to speak of the spirit of conservatism which seems to characterise the teaching of the Upanishads. This is, of course, very closely connected with their determinism and with the slight emphasis they lay upon the importance of the individual and of society. We can have no true belief in the progress of the individual unless we can believe also that the individual is worth improving, and is free both to bring about his own improvement and that of the society in which he lives.

As regards individual improvement, we may notice that determinism leaves no place for the feeling of subjective remorse, dissatisfaction, or divine discontent, which is the condition of all desire for progress. If we did not commit sins, or if they were committed simply by the spirit of the whole working through them, how could we be sorry for them. Regret or shame is altogether useless: these unfortunate occurrences simply had to be. Now this comfort which comes from a sense of irresponsibility for disastrous actions, though it may seem at first to be an optimistic gain, bringing peace of mind, soon passes over into dull and cold indifference

Such a temper is of course a barrier to progress, and it has also a hardening influence upon the mind which is not very far removed from despair. Is it not true of the best souls, at least, that they would often give anything to be able to break through the ice of indifference and be sorry for their misdeeds? In such sorrow there is a ray of hope—it is the "godly sorrow which worketh repentance." But if they can be only indifferent in regard to their failings, even the impulse which makes deliverance possible is taken away and nothing but dull acquiescence in present imperfections remains. Wakefulness of spirit is desirable even at the cost of pain, and there is no depression deeper than that of the soul who desires to feel sorrow for his sins against righteousness and fails even to feel this sorrow. If, further, we are trying to exert a moral influence upon another, we depend upon rousing in him a similar sense of shame and remorse. If, however, there is no warrant for this, as the philosophy we are considering would have us believe, our leverage is gone. Dissatisfaction, whether with ourselves or in regard to others, is the spring of all progress.

Passing from consideration of the absence of a feeling of remorse, we may look at the matter from a more objective point of view, and ask whether a belief in individual progress can be at all justified from the point of view of the Upanishads. When we take into account the determinism of the system, this question must be answered in the negative. It will surely be admitted that progress is possible only if the individual concerned desires to make it, but, if we are bound in the chain of the past, or if everything which we think we are doing is the inevitable action of the Divine unity, we are deprived of all incentive to action. An "icy cold breath," as Deussen puts it, has blown upon us and benumbed all our faculties. Our actions become merely recurrent exercises of the soul, serving no useful purpose, and the moral struggle becomes a meaningless process. Like the Eleatics, the teachers of the Upanishads sacrifice *becoming* to *being*, but in the moral sphere this attitude has disastrous consequences. We abandon the moral struggle, either because it is futile or because the result will inevitably be brought about independently of our striving. If, further, a final view of things allows no importance to the individual and admits no concrete and permanent individual character, the stimulus to progress on the part of the individual is taken away. In order that a man may put forth his most intense moral effort he must believe that his efforts count for something in the scheme of reality and that by means of them he can win something which will endure through all eternity. Thus, belief in individual progress seems to be bound up with belief in personal immortality. The thought of reunion with the divine is not enough to stimulate our efforts after return. We require a higher ideal, which will not compel us to sacrifice all that we have won by moral endeavour. Progress is meaningless if it ends in absorption, but conversely, unless we can believe in progress, absorption is the utmost that we desire.

We shall return to this connection between immortality and progress a little later. In the meantime, we may consider whether the Upanishads admit of any fuller belief in *world*-progress than in the progress of the individual. Now, if a man feels that he himself can make no real progress, he is not likely to attribute progress to the world as a whole. If he is wholly within the grasp of the past, or if he is the architect of his own fate only in the modified sense of passing on what he has received, he is not likely to conceive of the world in terms of the gradual embodiment of an ideal. If he cannot himself originate schemes of reform, but only seem to originate them, and if it is true that "movements towards reform and progress are due to personal initiative in the first instance," it is a short step to the belief that these schemes have no enduring value and that reality, as a whole, does not admit of them.

The spirit of this philosophy, in its more idealistic phase, does not admit of such attention to the world process as could invest it with the dignity of progress. If the whole process is in the last resort supremely unimportant, advance can lie only in the direction of a gradual realisation of this unimportance. There is no point in saying that the present is an improvement on the past, or is preparatory for a still better state of things in the future. It has often been remarked that in India the historical spirit is unusually deficient, but such deficiency is not to be wondered at, for why should we seek to understand the past, why should we seek to obtain guidance from it for the future, if past and future alike are parts of a meaningless round? Why should we spend our reforming efforts upon a totality which, as a whole, is without reality? Abstract idealism can permit no reform of the world, only an abandonment of it.

If, again, we fail in our idealistic endeavour, and find that the world refuses to be negated, can we get any nearer a conception of progress? It would seem rather that empirical reality, when it is asserted to be *merely* empirical reality, will present itself to us as a huge insoluble problem. We shall be overwhelmed with a sense of "cosmic discouragement." We have taken the reason out of the world and left it as a meaningless mass, which yet oppresses us continually with its problems. We have failed to explain the world, and all that seems left to us to do is to abandon it.

Even when we refuse to carry our abstract idealism to the extreme of negation, and, accepting the permission of certain interpreters of the Upanishads, allow within our philosophy and "for practical purposes" a subordinate reality to the world, can we form a conception of progress? This question also must be answered in the negative. The general effect of the position taken up is simply to deify the existing state of things, or the inevitable consequences of the existing state. We must not suppose that we can do anything to alter the course of events. If the universe is divine, it would seem almost impious to regard it as either requiring or susceptible of change. Already it is perfect, at least with a potentiality which does not require our efforts in order to turn it into an actuality. If we have doubts about this perfection we should remember our ignorance, and conceive it as at least possible that there is no such thing as evil, and that the appearance of it is due solely to our extremely partial view of the whole.

Process, there no doubt is, but it is only of a cyclic character—a returning ever and again to the point of departure. There may be many series of such processes in the illimitable succession of the centuries, but there will be no advance. Each later cycle will resemble the earlier, in meaningless repetition, and in the end all things will be as they were in the beginning.

The consequences of this denial of world-progress are depressing in various ways. In the first place it deepens our sense of bondage. It might have seemed reasonable to sacrifice our individual liberty to the working of the whole, if we could have been sure that in the whole some purpose was being worked out. But to surrender ourselves to a process is a renunciation without compensation.

Again, the denial of progress seems to deprive us of the element of value which the pantheistic explanations of pain and evil seem to possess. Suffering, e.g., has often been explained as sacrifice for the good of the whole, but sacrifice is unmeaning in an unprogressive world. It serves no purpose. Neither in such a world can we explain physical suffering as necessary for the moral education of the individual. If moral progress is ultimately both impossible and unnecessary, there is no place for such agencies as may be expected to promote it. Further, in regard to the problem of evil, we might be more willing to agree that evil was necessary for growth, or that, when viewed in connection with the whole, it was no evil, if we could see that some plan for the whole was being worked out. But when such insight is denied us, when we find that what we have to acquiesce in is the position of evil in this present world, or in a future world which will be in no way an improvement upon this one, then the last remnant of our comfort is gone. The ever-recurring demand of the human soul is that evil shall be regarded as *abnormal*, that it shall have an end. We cannot permanently acquiesce in its inevitableness. It must be dealt with by way of progress towards better things if we are to be saved from pessimism.

Finally, we come to the most depressing consequence of all—the denial of world-progress paralyses human activity. The subjective effect of such a denial is a sense of futility, and the futile is unworthy of human endeavour. In the *Kaushitaki Upanishad* we get this advice: "Let no man try to find out what action is, let him know the agent" (III-8), and the advice is but too readily taken. Why should we act in reference to a world which is meaningless, or in reference to a reality which will give no permanent place to the results of our highest efforts. Indian writers often refuse to face the issue here, and remind us that the noblest souls do not desire the "fruit of works." There is no question here of desiring the fruit of works in the form of material rewards, but there is a question—and an unavoidable question—as to the usefulness or uselessness of works in the highest sense. If the denial of progress involves that all work is in the last resort a futile endeavour, the effect of this doctrine is, without doubt, paralysing and depressing. We may not desire reward in the shape of pleasure, but it is difficult to undergo labour and trouble, to offer the sacrifice of renunciation, while all the time we have the consciousness that the life both of ourselves and others is supremely unimportant. It is more than difficult, it is impossible, for it is contrary to human nature. The Upanishads themselves recognise this. The *Aitariya* tells us: "Whatever a man reaches he wishes to go beyond" (III, 3-1). If we are simply adrift on the stream of becoming, and if the stream leads nowhere in particular, if as things have been so they will be, on and on, without progress, we ask despairingly; "What is the use of it all?" The universality of the reach of the pantheistic conception swallows up the importance of the individual, and mere cyclic processes have a satiating effect upon us—"a like event happeneth to all." Under the influence of the innate impulsive activity of human nature, we may indeed initiate new schemes, but we have not the power of continuance. Soon there comes to us the paralysing thought that all this has happened before, and that any improvement there may seem to be is but temporary. Soon we shall be once more where we were at the beginning. Those who are interested in Indian reforms have often had to lament the spasmodic character of the efforts put forth, and Indians themselves are amongst the first to point out that, while there are many new beginnings, steady continuance is not so frequent a phenomenon. This failure in constructive social effort may be connected directly with the aspect of the Indian philosophy we have just been considering. The insufficient attention to the world and the denial of progress in the world, even when it is attended to, have had a benumbing effect upon the national energies, and have thus produced an atmosphere of pessimism. We demand an ideal beyond the present, an ideal of fulness of life, which shall serve as the ground not only of the good which now is but of all that which is to be. If this demand of the human spirit is ignored, if we are told that as things have been so they will be, we sink down under the feeling of inevitableness. Pessimism and gloomy conservatism are the inevitable consequences. There ensues a contemplative attitude of indifference, but indifference if persisted in results in what has been called "cataleptic insensibility," a relapse into vacuity of interest and poverty of purpose. Progress is essential to optimism, and conversely optimism is essential to progress. If, therefore, we would have progress, we must generate an atmosphere of optimism.

This we can do only by falling back upon the principle of self-conservation, not in any selfish sense but as a joyous trust in the existence which has been given to us. We must take this at its full value, and if we do this we cannot believe in its annihilation or absorption. This brings us back to the question of immortality, and the relation of this belief to a belief in progress, individual or universal. Whether the individual soul might hope for continued existence was one of the points of controversy between Sankara and Ramanuja. It would seem that Sankara, who denies immortality, can claim to be a more faithful interpreter of the general teaching of the Upanishads. There are, indeed, certain passages in the Upanishads in which it is suggested that the individual soul dwells for ever in a paradise in which its individuality is maintained. Cf. *Kaushitaki Upanishad* II, 15, where we read that "the enlightened man goes to heaven where the gods are, and having reached this, he who knows this, becomes immortal with the immortality which the gods enjoy." There is here no hint of the destruction of individuality, and the whole of this particular Upanishad is in much the same strain. Nevertheless, even if in certain cases the writers of the Upanishads are disposed to grant immortality to individuals, they do so in a way which leaves their abstract pantheism ultimately undisturbed. The comparison of the highest state to dreamless sleep is suggestive, and the metaphor of rivers running into the sea produces the same impression of acquiescence in the destruction of individuality.

We need not be surprised at this slightness of the craving for immortality, for why would we desire to continue within a system which has itself no meaning and presents no opportunity for progress? The sooner we get rid of such existence the better. But we may ask, Has there not been action and reaction here, between the denial of immortality and the denial of progress, and why should not this action and reaction be raised to a higher plane and become productive of optimism rather than of pessimism? Let us emphasise all the hints of the importance and permanence of the individual which our nature may give us. Let us, we say again, trust the existence God has given us and believe in the worth of our own personality. Then we shall understand the possibility of progress in our own character, and not only the possibility but the actuality, and, taking our stand upon this, we shall attribute progress to the world also, for now the world contains elements which are worth bringing to perfection, and which refuse annihilation and absorption. We are now able to conceive of an ideal beyond the actual, which shall show its ultimate reality not by negation of the actual but by conservation of the good and victory over the evil that is in the actual, and which shall tell us of the souls of just men made perfect, who may live in utter harmony and communion with the Supreme Spirit, the Father and Lord of all.

CHAPTER VI

The Need of Theism and the Message of Christianity

IT now remains for us to gather up the results of our enquiry, and indicate what help we may receive from the Upanishads towards the formulation of an ideal of life. In what direction does the teaching of the Upanishads require to be supplemented and modified, in order to meet more effectively the religious needs of humanity?

In the preceding chapters we have indicated the importance of the Upanishads and their place in the historical development of Indian thought. We have attempted to show the form in which the religious problem presented itself to the thinkers whose doctrines are contained in these sacred books. We have indicated the general nature of the solution offered, and come to the conclusion that this solution is at once pantheistic and pessimistic. In the last two chapters we have been occupied with an investigation into the peculiar characteristics of the solution which seem to explain the resulting pessimistic outlook upon life. We shall now ask whether it may not be possible to arrive at a view of life which will conserve all that is of value in the teaching of the Upanishads and at the same time avoid the dangerous consequences which we have seen are likely to result from that teaching?

We have described these consequences as, on the whole, pessimistic, and the consideration of the nature of the bliss which is associated with the highest religious ideal has not compelled us to alter this description to any material extent. Now, if any system of thought results in a pessimistic view of life, such a consequence inclines us to doubts regarding the adequacy of the system. For pessimism is an implicit accusation. It is a hint that the universe is proceeding on mistaken lines, it is a suggestion of abnormality, a failure to supply an explanation of certain anomalies. From this point of view a system which lands us in pessimism stands self-condemned, or, if we do not care to put the matter so strongly as this, we can at least demand that such a system shall not be accepted until all other possible solutions have been examined and found wanting. Here is a challenge to further enquiry.

In proceeding to such an enquiry, however, we must not leave behind us the elements of value which are to be found in the teaching of the Upanishads. Though the principle of negation is carried to an extreme in this teaching, yet, it has distinct places in the development of the moral and religious life. We cannot win our souls simply by following the natural impulses of our nature. Sometimes narrow is the way and strait is the gate that leadeth unto life. We can win our souls only through much renunciation of the easy and the pleasant. If the hand or the foot offend, they must be cut off, so that, even though halt and maimed, we may yet find entrance into the kingdom. The Indian ascetic has distinctly a lesson to teach the easy-going pleasure-seeker of modern times. The mistake lies not in the negation, but in making negation the whole of the matter. The principle of asceticism, when carried to extremes, involves a reprehensible distrust of life. Deep down in the philosopy of the Upanishads this distrust of existence lies. We find it shadowed forth in the doctrine of *tapás* (Cf. *Mundaka* I, 1-8) which is elevated into a principle of creation, but which does not thereby lose altogether the meaning of self-coercion or renunciation. We find it permeating the whole doctrine of *maya.* We find it practically in the self-mutilations of the Yogi and in the "one-pointed" contemplative absorption of the mystic. In all these phases of thought and practice there is always evident the tendency to spread renunciation to the whole of existence, to think that the world is wholly evil because it gives us the opportunity of doing evil, to wish to destroy all our human impulses because some of them are the occasions of temptation. The axe is laid to the root of a tree which would yet be capable of bearing fruit if only its unduly luxuriant branches were pruned. But the mistake of this extreme of treatment must not hide from us the necessity of pruning. It is in this thought, when transferred from the region of metaphor to the life of the spirit, that the value of negation lies. Further, we must recognise the lesson of seriousness which the Upanishads teach us. We have seen that the form of their main life-problem was due to an intense and vivid consciousness of the sorrow of the world, of the vanity and impermanence of all mundane things. We have seen also that the gloom in which the problem originated was not easily shaken off, and coloured the solution to an unjustifiable extent. Nevertheless, we must not, because of our abhorrence of gloomy conclusions, rush to the opposite extreme and indulge in a facile optimism. We must not light-heartedly gloss over the pain and evil of the world. If our lines have been cast in pleasant places, we must still remember the sorrow of our neighbours. If temptations have not overwhelmed us, if, because, of favouring circumstances, it may be, we have not fallen into grievous sins such as the world may mark, we must yet remember that with others the struggle has been a sore one, and sometimes the end has been, not victory, but defeat. We must not forget the change in our destiny that the years may bring. We must not be so captivated by the pleasure of to-day as to forget the possible pain of to-morrow, nor so lulled to sleep by present security as to forget that almost immediately we may find ourselves in the forefront of the battle, fighting against overwhelming odds for the purity of our souls and the righteousness of our lives. The blind, selfish, superficial, momentary existence can afford no solution of the problems of life. We must go forth to meet the sorrow of the world and of our destiny, before we can hope to deal with that sorrow. He only is secure who is prepared for whatever the future may bring him. We cannot be prepared unless we realise all the possibilities, the sombre as well as the glad, the distressing as well as the comforting, the dangerous as well as the safe. The surgeon must probe deeply before he can hope to cure the dangerous wound: so must we go deep down into the ills of life before we can apply the remedy. Lightheartedness must be balanced by serious-mindedness, and in emphasising the latter the the Upanishads teach us a lesson that should not be forgotten. We should estimate also at its full value the other great contribution which they make to religious thought in their doctrine of monism and the identity of the human and divine. They have laid in this doctrine the speculative basis of mysticism, and more and more religion is tending in a mystical direction. The idea of a God at a distance from the world, working upon an intractable matter which is the source of evil, or setting in motion a vast mechanism with which He need no longer actively concern Himself, is alien to our thought. We demand that God should be in the world and in us. We feel that He is not far from any one of us, and that in Him we live and move and have our being. We emphasise the community of nature between the human and the divine. We are not separate, self-centred, independent beings, but divinity is within us and round about us. We desire to feel that God is all in all, and that we may abandon ourselves to His all-comprehending Being. Towards such a feeling the pantheistic doctrine of identity, as set forth in the Upanishads, certainly helps us onwards, and in so doing performs an essentially religious function. Pantheism, as has been said, "challenges Christianity to make the most of its monotheisn."[1] It summons us, in all our formulation of the conception of the one and only God, to hold fast to the unity of humanity with the divine.

Yet we have found that the aspect of this unity which the Upanishads present to us is inadequate to express the religious relationship. Such a relationship involves essentially two terms, and loses its content if the two terms are merged into one. The conception of identity, whatever degree of closeness of com-

[1] Clarke, *Christian Doctrine of God*, p. 276.

munion it may seem to promise, really destroys the possibility of communion altogether. The individual between whom and God the communion is supposed to exist is either denied all value or is indistinguishably merged in the totality of the being of God. The unity of God is of such a character as to exclude all diversity. Therefore, if we are to retain any character it must be at the expense of the being of God. In other words, we have reached the dilemma that if God is, we are not; if we are, God is not. All freedom and initiative have been taken away from the individual, and his personality has resolved itself into a shadowy mist.

This result we have found to be due to the abstract procedure of intellectualism, and we must therefore modify our exclusive devotion to this procedure, not by way of reaction to the extreme of scepticism and emotionalism, but by transformation and supplement. We must accept the warning against "exalting the cultivation of the critical and logical faculties to a position of undue eminence."[1] We must press home upon the thought of the Upanishads the ideal which is sketched by Pundit S. N. Tattvabhushan—"Knowledge is not mere intellectual inferential knowledge, but a state of lasting enlightenment, a never-failing light, illumining all departments of conscious life—colouring the sensuous perceptions, guiding the judgments, touching the feelings, controlling the desires, and determining the decisions of the conscience."[2] It must be an intellect which guides the feelings and does not abandon them to their own impulsive force. It must also be in close connection with character, and, to use Meredith's phrase, "incur the immense debtorship for a thing done." It must not lose itself in sentimental contemplation, but recognise that all knowledge involves an active response on our part. It must, in short, correspond to the conception of the intellect which a recent scholar has attributed to Socrates. It must be "a certain over-mastering principle or power, which lays hold

[1] Mazumdar, *Brahma-Samaj*, p. 136,

[2] *Hindu Theism*, p. 115.

primarily of the intellect, but, through the intellect, of the entire personality, moulding and disciplining the will and the emotions into absolute unity with itself, a principle from which courage, temperance, justice and all other virtues inevitably flow".[1]

It is only by thus widening our idea of the intellect, emphasising its active character, and making it practically the expression of our whole personality in its higher and more spiritual exercise, that we can escape from the *impasse* in which the abstract philosophy of identity has landed us. In attempting to understand the religious relationship, we must keep faithful to the fundamental principle of all experience whatsoever. This principle is the relation of subject and object—the assertion of a duality within a unity. Knowledge cannot be explained by identifying ourselves with that which we would know. The subject and object, however congenial to one another and however closely they may be united in the unity of knowledge, must yet remain distinct. And the relation between them is a relation of co-operation. Truth is not a mere passive pouring in of impressions upon our souls. The truths which we obtain are hypotheses for action, and are proved to be truths by the fact that they permit of action in an orderly and systematic manner. Notice that we do not hold the very prevalent doctrine that truth is truth simply because it enables us to act. Mere action is not enough. Truth is rather truth because it enables us to act in an *orderly and systematic* manner. The truths which make this action possible prove their claim as descriptive of a system of reality. But the point of this digression into metaphysics is to bring out the fact that knowledge is essentially co-operation, involving a distinction within the unity of subject and object.

We must carry this consideration with us when we attempt to think of God. He must be the highest Object of all our thinking, and our relation to Him must be one of communion, not of absorption. No doubt

---

[1] Adam's *Religious Teachers of Greece*, p. 329.

there are certain dangers in thinking of God as Object. There is the danger, e.g., of comparing Him in our minds to the objects of sense. The philosophy of the Upanishads seeks to avoid such dangers by thinking of Him as the Universal Subject, and such a mode of conception is also useful as emphasing the spiritual kinship between God and us. But God must also be regarded as Object. Only thus can He be understood, only thus can He be worshipped, only thus can He be loved.

To take the last mentioned aspect first—love is impossible on the basis of mere identity. We may speak of the intellectual love of God, as Spinoza did, but this can mean only the thinking over again of the ideas of God, unless we can conserve on the one hand the individual who is to love and the Divine Object who is to be loved. Love is a relation between two terms, and the relation cannot be maintained if the two terms are fused together into an identity. It is a going forth in sympathy towards the being of another, and it is essential that there should be that other. Similarly with the relation of worship. It implies a going forth beyond ourselves, a concentration of feelings of devotion and adoration upon a Divine Being from whom we all the time distinguish ourselves. We cannot worship ourselves; neither, if we are merged in the object of our adoration, can *we* render to the Object the homage which all worship includes. So the distinctness of the subject-object relation is the basis of the essentially religious impulses of love and adoration.

We have said also that only thus can God be understood. We have seen that the intellectualism of the Upanishads ended in a confession of intellectual bankruptcy. No predicates could be applied to God in the ordinary use of the word predicate. The ultimate conclusion was a negation—*neti, neti*—it is not so, it is not so. And we have seen also that this refusal of knowledge led to a swing of the pendulum in the direction of emotionalism and riotous imagination. Mysticism has always been liable to this extreme of emotionalism, unrestrained imagination and scepticism. When the barrenness of the intellect has been revealed, the soul has comforted itself with a religion of mere feeling. Rationalism has given place in modern times to romanticism, and to-day we are confronted with the anti-intellectualism of the Bergsonian philosophy. Now we maintain that this extreme of reaction is unnecessary. We do not wish for a moment to forget the warning which is conveyed in emotional theology against the impertinent use of our intellectual faculties or the misapplication of the categories of science. We cannot, by searching, find out God, we cannot comprehend Him within the narrow range of our logical conceptions. The lesson of humility should be well learnt. But at the same time, humility does not mean distrust, and, if it does have this meaning, a reason for the distrust has to be supplied. Such a reason may be found in the consideration that the intellect, in giving such a prominent place to the principle of identity, has made its own task impossible. It has divorced itself from the ordinary conditions of experience, and so its experience cannot bring forth the fruit of knowledge. If, in order to know a thing, we must *be* that thing, then all knowledge is for ever impossible. So, many of the mystics have submitted to what they thought was inevitable, and have said that God cannot be known except by way of the feelings. But this doctrine of the impotence of knowledge is not a necessary consequence of the mystical position. It is only a consequence of the failure of the mystic to take account of objectivity. Mystical experience does not necessarily float in the air, reaching forth to nothing beyond its own emotions. It has a relation to ultimate truth, and the aim of the highest type of mystic has always been to reach that *truth*. As has been said, "Mysticism, if it be not a real communion of the human soul with a Beyond which is a supreme objective fact and not a mere subjective ideal, is nothing." We must fully recognise the existence of this objective fact, and we must use the intellect to investigate its nature. The *neti, neti* of the Upanishads must not be ultimate, but only an expression of humility and of dissatisfaction with the conclusions which have *as yet* been obtained.

We thus find that the intellect is of no avail in the service of religion, unless it keeps rigidly to the fundamental condition of the subject-object relation, but that, when used with due observance of this condition, it may be trusted to bring us into contact with ultimate truth. In fact, its use in even the smallest affairs of practical life implies a consciousness of an ultimate standard of truth, and encourages us in the belief that the secrets of the Divine are to some extent accessible to our human thought. We cannot say that the simplest statement is true, without thereby testifying to a standard of truth and putting forward a claim to some appreciation of that standard. The intellect, if normally exercised, is of use religiously, and normal exercise implies that God and man, though possessing community of nature, yet remain distinct with a distinctness analogous to that of subject and object in ordinary experience. In other words, a normal use of the intellect and a true appreciation of its range and power leads us to the confines of theism.

We find that a proper understanding of the moral needs of man leads us in the same direction. The Upanishads have emphasised the human sense of need and the existence of aspirations after a better life. They have granted that whatever a man reaches he wishes to go beyond, but they have not fully appreciated the significance of this fundamental craving in human nature, and the closeness of contact with reality which the moral life indicates.

There are two possible ways of interpreting the moral progress of the individual or of humanity. We may look upon this progress as a revelation of reality or as a growing consciousness of unreality, i.e., as leading us towards something or leading us away from something, as positive or negative. The Upanishads on the whole adopt the latter procedure. For them morality is an exercise of the soul, having as its chief end the loosening of the bonds which attach us to the ordinary world. It is a deadening down of the activities of the soul, a destruction of its desires. Thus, by emptying our life of all contents we may be the more ready for that identification of the human and the divine which is the goal set before us in this teaching. Now it is obvious that such a procedure does not distinguish between the life and the death of the soul. We are told that by exercising our moral capacities we purify our souls from the earthly, but we might just as readily reach this end by withdrawal from action altogether and by refusal to use the moral powers which we possess. But the important point for us to notice here is, that morality cannot be expected to throw any light upon the character of the reality which we hope to reach by means of it. By the time we are in contact with this reality, morality has itself disappeared. The Upanishads, at least, do not allow us to carry moral predicates with us to the highest reality, they do not allow us to attribute goodness or holiness or righteousness to God.

But is this refusal a necessary one? May not moral progress be illuminative in a positive manner? Are we not, in all our moral struggle, continually in contact with reality. The simplest deed that we do has a character of irrevocableness about it which creates in us the feeling that we are dealing with fundamental reality. When once we have done a deed, nothing can change that deed. It is done for ever, inexorably. We are not dealing with fancies here, but with facts. Similarly, the distinction between right and wrong seems to be a fundamental one. Unless the conscience is perverted there is, in the doing of what we clearly know to be right from the moral point of view (which position the Upanishads would allow us provisionally to occupy), a feeling of harmony with reality which seems to be a revelation. We feel that Reality admits of, and accepts, our deed, and that in the doing of it our eyes have been opened to the truth of existence. Take, again, the universal craving in the human soul for the *better*, simply for the *better*. Does it mean nothing? Does it not mean at the very least that we have a consciousness of good beyond that which we have already attained to? And this again has a double implication.

It means that we refuse that acquiescence in the actual which some phases of naturalistic pantheism would encourage us in, but it means also that, on the other hand, we cling firmly to the belief that there is a reality beyond the present actuality which shall justify our belief in goodness and provide the possibility of the realisation of it. Our consciousness of the better demands an ascending scale of values, which shall culminate in one Supreme Value. Seeing that such a Supreme Value is necessary to explain even the faintest moral aspiration, we may assert, by a not unjustifiable exercise of faith, what has been already described as the "identity of value and existence." We demand that "there shall never be one lost good." We interpret the ultimate reality rather in terms of worth than in terms of mere totality of existence, and we hold that the idea of worth is a contradictory idea unless it includes the idea of existence. We hold that nothing can be regarded as supremely valuable unless it has also a place in the scheme of ultimate existence, and that, more positively, wherever there is a belief in a Supreme Value there is also a belief in the existence of that Supreme Value. We must not be taken to mean that in a purely arbitrary manner we may form a conception of something as good, and forthwith demand that this good should have existence. Our argument rests on the fundamental and general character of the moral consciousness, upon the desire for the "better" which is inalienable from humanity. We hold that the "better" implies the "best", and that we cannot pass even the simplest moral judgment without thereby assuming that the Supreme Reality possesses moral character. One moral judgment leads on to another in an endless chain. We continually ask why a thing or an act is good. One answer leads on to another question, and the final "why" can be answered only by an assertion of the goodness of God. It is not a dogmatic assertion—our argument is that the first moral question in the chain of question and answer implies the last moral answer.

Of course, from the point of view of the Upanishads it may be contended that this argument is invalid for the simple reason that existence is not a blessing but a curse. Existence may be a diminution of value rather than an enhancement of it. Therefore, we are not at liberty to argue that the Highest Good necessarily includes existence, or to think that we make goodness any more goodness by attaching existence to it. To this contention we may reply, in the first place, that the followers of the Upanishads do not ultimately deny the value of existence. Their assertion that existence is an evil would apply only to what they would call empirical existence. The whole aim of their teaching is to show how we may attain to communion with a reality which indubitably exists. Alongside of this admission of the value of existence, which we may justifiably extract from their teaching, we put the ordinary human moral consciousness. We hold that the sheer force of logic demands that whoever believes in an ultimate reality of any kind, and at the same time is a moral being, must unite the two ideas of goodness and of reality. Or, in the second place, we may put the matter less abstractly, and simply deny the implication that existence generally, whether empirical or transcendental, is on the whole a curse rather than a blessing. The ground of our denial is that such procedure is abnormal, as has been already pointed out, and the *prima facie* evidence is in favour of the normal. To attach the idea of existence, then, to the idea of goodness is not to detract from goodness but rather to increase it, and if this be so, then it follows that the Supremely Valuable, whose value by hypothesis cannot be further increased, must already include existence; in other words, we may apply moral predicates to God. But if our moral consciousness leads on to the idea of God as possessing moral qualities, we must conceive of God as personal. For we cannot think of morality except as the characteristic of a personal being. It consists in conscious activity, and conscious activity is unintelligible except in connection with personality. And we are encouraged in thus attributing personality to God, if we hold fast to our belief in the ultimate identity of Value and Existence. For personality is our most valuable possession, and we can think of the ultimately valuable only in terms of the highest value we know. We may find also some support in the place which the idea of a personal God holds in the universal religious consciousness. We have found that even within the system of thought which has been dominated by the Upanishads, discontent has been frequently expressed with a God who is merely impersonal. "The worship of the impersonal laid no hold upon my heart," says Tulsidas, and he is but echoing the feelings and interpreting the practice of multitudes who have been searching their hearts and finding in the fulness of their personality the revelation of God.

Thus the intellectual necessity of being faithful to the fundamental condition of all experience, viz., the subject-object relation, combined with the attempt to satisfy the demands of the moral consciousness, including the consciousness of the supreme value of personality, lead us to a theistic position. It is only in such a conception of God, as at once immanent in the world and transcendent over it, that we can find anything to meet those needs of human nature which the Upanishads have revealed to us, but failed to satisfy. We found that they were able to deal with the problem of the pain and evil of the world only by negating the world or by regarding it as the manifestation of a process leading to no end. It was a mere process and not a progress, and it swept into its universal movement all human individuality and freedom, holding out no hope of personal continuance nor of ultimate victory. To deny the world is, however, to run away from the problem rather than to solve it, and to deprive man of freedom and the hope of permanence and continuance is to do violence to his nature. We need a conception of God which will preserve the reality of the world, take full account of the pain and evil that is in it, and yet hold out the hope of progress, both for the world and the individuals in it. Through all stages of the progress, and in any conception of the ultimate consummation, man must be allowed to retain the freedom and the value of his personalty. Such a conception we may find in theism. One of the most frequently quoted texts in the Christian scriptures is, "God so loved the world that He gave his only begotten Son, that whosoever believeth in Him should not perish, but should have everlasting life." We might very profitably take this verse as our guide in the few reflections which still fall to be made. It contains the deepest truths of philosophy as well as of religion.

First of all, it suggests an illuminating view of the true relation between God and the world. The world which God has created is not a mere play of His fancy. He has taken up an attitude of seriousness to it. Between Him and it there exists a real relation, such a relation as is implied in the ordinary use of the word *love*—a relation of reciprocity. We must not think that this reciprocity involves anything approaching equality, as if God and the universe stood over against each other, entirely dualistically, in the equality of action and reaction. God is much more than adequate to the universe which He has made. There is in Him a reserve of fulness and of power which is by no means exhausted in the work of creation. The sense of need which is inherent in humanity shows that the universe is not complete and self-contained in itself, and religious experience gives further assurance that beyond the finite universe there are the infinite riches of God. God has limited Himself in creating the world, but the important point to notice is that He trusts the world which He has made. It is more than a mere thought. It has been given such reality that He would not be God without it. In a sense He is now a finite God, as limited by the Universe He has made. As Ward puts it, "The term 'Finite God,' as accepted by true theists, means for them all that God can mean, if God implies the world and is not a God without it; it means a living God with a living world, not a potter God with a world of illusory clay, not an inconceivable God that is only infinite and absolute, because, it is beyond everything and means nothing."[1] The evidence of God's trust

[1] *Pluralism and Theism*, p. 444.

in the world and His love towards it lies in the fact that He has created a *living* world and not a world of "illusory clay," i.e., a world which is either a dream or is real only with the reality of dead matter. God's limitation, it must be remembered, is not a limitation imposed upon Him by some fate or force. It is a self-limitation and the manner of the limitation is that He has breathed into the universe the breath of life, and, most of all, that He has created self-conscious beings. It is only thus that we can properly distinguish between creation and a mere evolution iand unfolding. Sometimes it is said that the main implication of creation, as distinct from emanation, is that God could have acted otherwise if He had so chosen, but the emphasis should rather be put on the self-subsistence of that which is created. As Lotze has it, "A thing which was not conscious of itself, and which did not feel or in some fashion or other enjoy what we might call being for itself, would never be anything more than a selfless state of the Creator, and there would be nothing by which it could be distinguished from the reality which it already has as a thought of God."[1] Unless we can emphasise this idea that creation consists pre-eminently in the bringing into existence of self-conscious beings, the unity of God will swallow up the difference, and the assertion of God will mean either the negation of the world or the identification of God with its totality.

A favourite way of putting the matter in modern philosophy is to say, that creation is unintelligible unless it involves the creation of creators. The universe is made up of self-conscious centres of initiation, and the method of development which God has chosen is to give to these creators freedom of action and self-determination. We must take the fact of human existence as we find it, and man is less than man if he is not creative. This conception does not mean that God has surrendered His influence over men or His general direction of the world, but it means that He must not interpret this direction in any mechanical

---

[1] *Phil. of Religion*, p. 95.

way which would interfere with human liberty and personality. Neither, in our attempt to rise above mechanical conceptions, are we at liberty to speak of the consciousness of God as including or penetrating human consciousness. Such an idea would be subversive of the very idea of consciousness, for consciousness means nothing unless it means existence for oneself. No, the conception we are considering rather means that the relation between God and man must be regarded as one of co-operation. God contributes indeed the original impulse, but He does so in the form of "urgency or forward push," and not in the way of compulsion. Perhaps the analogy of literary collaboration might throw light on the relation. The predominant partner in the collaboration may contribute the inspiration and a certain amount of guidance, but he does not do so in such a way as to destroy the free activity of the other partner.

Thus the primary love of God to the world is shown in His creation of *creative* beings, and the universe is real because of them and for them. This emphasis upon the reality of creation carries with it important consequences. It enables us first of all to see the untruth of asceticism, if asceticism is carried further than is necessary for the purposes of moral discipline. Asceticism of an extreme type involves a condemnation of the world, but how can we entirely condemn a world which God has made, has really made? As Meredith puts it, "Earth is not forgotten for a moment as a vehicle for the knowledge of God." It is given to us rather to enjoy, to appreciate, to use, not necessarily to accept in its totality as giving us completeness of guidance, but certainly to value as the sphere of God's working. There may be in it a mystery of pain and evil, but for these there are certain obvious remedies also provided in the reforming activity of man under the protecting care of God, and until we have fully used these remedies we cannot dismiss the problem of pain and evil as insoluble.

Further, emphasis upon the reality of the universe, and especially upon the reality of human activity, means that history is given its proper value. The development of the universe is real and not a mere play of fancy. We have seen that, on the principles of the Upanishads, it was found impossible to derive any guidance from history, and the influence of these principles has resulted in the comparative absence of the historical spirit in India. On general grounds this attitude might seem to be foreign to human nature. Is not poetry full of references to the value of the past, to possibilities of mounting "on stepping stones of their dead selves", to the "increasing purpose" of the ages? Philosophical contempt for history is all the more surprising in a country like India, where tradition holds such undisputed sway. The contradiction can only mean that facts have been too strong for the philosophy. The force of history has been felt even while its reality is denied, and, as happens in all cases where theory and practice are divorced, the unrationalised facts have acquired an excessive influence. But surely we ought rather to bring our theory into agreement with the facts, and attempt to understand and value the facts by means of it. History has reality as the record of the activity of man and the guidance of God, and is worthy of study in order that we may learn from it how in the future we may advance beyond the past. We may perhaps find that in history we have the chief revelation of God.

Another consequence of allowing reality to the world development may be noted. It makes incarnation possible. Incarnation is essentially the entrance of the divine into the world-development. But if this latter has no reality, then incarnation is logically impossible. It has always seemed a curious contradiction that belief in incarnation should be so enormously prevalent in a country where the predominant philosophy does not permit of it. The contrast is very similar to that with which we dealt in the last paragraph, and may be explained in much the same way, as a more or less unconscious retention of incompatible views. We may notice also that the absence of a proper appreciation of the historical probably explains the peculiar character of Indian belief in incarnations, viz., the prodigious number of objects to which this belief attaches. On the other hand a proper appreciation of history would provide a remedy in two ways. It would both supply a basis for an adequate theory of incarnation and, by setting up barriers of fact, would restrain the imagination from running riot in the construction of deities numerous enough to represent every passing whim and fancy.

We have yet to show more fully how this emphasis upon human freedom helps us in the understanding of pain and evil, gives us the promise of progress and immortality. If God and man are in co-operation, then all the evil and the pain cannot be ascribed to God. May we not find the explanation of much of it in the way in which man has misused his freedom? Moreover, we must not simply rely upon God to put matters right, in the self-determination of man lies one of the main remedies. The exercise of this freedom gives further the joy of creative activity and the promise of continuance which is immortality. It is the basis also of moral and social reform. Ultimately belief in progress means belief in God as the home of all values—the guarantee that progress will culminate in something which is not now but which assuredly will be.

We may emphasise the difference between the pantheistic and the theistic treatment of the topic we have alluded to in the last paragraph. Take once more the problem of pain. Strictly speaking, the idealistic phase of the Upanishad philosophy would lead us to treat pain as an unreality, but this unreality rather refers to the sphere in which pain lies, and the explanation which deals more closely with the detailed facts of pain is that pain must be connected with the idea of fate. The individual has no rights over against the whole in which he is placed. But with the widening of sympathy and the deepening of the moral consciousness pain becomes more the problem of the single life. We cannot disregard its connection with our own individuality, nor can we disregard its connection with others also as individuals. The only explanation of pain which is satisfactory is that it should be seen to contribute to the permanent welfare of ourselves and others as *individuals*. We receive comfort only if, over against our present unhappiness, we can put a sense of our permanent value in the sight of God. Further, even if we were able to annihilate in thought the rights of our own personality and suffer for the good of the whole, pantheism is unable to supply us with an adequate motive for this resignation. Before we can be persuaded to suffer for the good of the whole we must believe that the whole is ultimately good. But for pantheism the ultimate reality is characterless. So we immediately ask the question, Why should we suffer? And we can receive an answer only if we can conceive of God as the ultimate reality of goodness and can regard ourselves as suffering present trials partly for the sake of the development of our own true and permanent personality, and partly in order that others may enter along with us into permanent ethical communion with God.

But when we have established our belief in the goodness of God, we must be careful to free it from pantheistic implications. We must not regard this goodness as already realised by us, or even as the inevitable outcome of a process in regard to which we have no responsibility. Pantheism makes, it might be said, too rapid a journey to the end of things, and also misinterprets the process by which that end is reached. Theism, on the other hand, takes what might be called a cross section of actuality, and while revealing the true state of things reveals also elements of hope. It avoids the extreme of deification of the actual and at the same time encourages us to act in accordance with our sense of responsibility by emphasising our own freedom and the possibility of progress which the universe allows. Goodness is not yet a reality as regards the actual state of the world, but it may become a reality. Theism gives us faith in a reality beyond the actual, which by its contrast with the actual will correspond to the contrast between the ideal and real implied in our moral consciousness, and will at the same time permit a faith in the possible realisation of the ideal.

By means of theism we reach à faith in God not only as the ground of the being of the world, but as the end of its being; who *is* in Himself, but who yet *is to be* as regards the realisation of Himself in the world. We cannot be satisfied with mere development or mere process. Development by itself and without purpose is an unmeaning term and has no religious value. As Lotze says, "Development does not satisfy the claims of religion, for development implies that outside the being that develops there is a universal order or circle of supreme laws, which determine in a general way the second state of this being."[1]

Now these eternal laws, which are above the things which develop and constitute what we mean by purpose, must be contained as ideas in a Supreme Mind. This mind is the real embodiment of the ideal, and in the God whose being it describes the whole process of the world finds that meaning which we signify by the word progress. And we must emphasise still more strongly the danger of the other pantheistic implication, viz., that this ideal for the world can be realised without the exercise of our freedom. God has entered into *co-operation* with mankind and He will not destroy that co-operation by taking our burden upon Himself. We not only depend upon God, but God depends on us. To introduce the ideal without such dependence on the help of man would be to defeat the purpose of God, for that purpose is the development and completion of a world of free personalities, and not the elaboration of a number of machines, however ingenious and perfect. But the perfection of human character is the crown of human effort, and cannot be attained except by means of that effort. Again, theism not only states the need of effort, but allows and emphasises its possibility. It thus has not the pessimistic consequence of stating a need which it does not at the same time suggest a way of supplying.

In short, we may say that in its practical view of the world theism avoids the pantheistic extremes of superficial optimism and unrelieved pessimism. It

[1] *Philosophy of Religion*, p. 136.

neither shuts its eyes to the pain and evil in the world, nor does it regard these elements as inevitable. It does not assert, on the one hand, that there is nothing to forgive, or, on the other, that forgiveness is impossible. Pfleiderer, in discussing the value of Christian theism, very well brings out this secure intermediate position of theism in general: "The Christian view of the world proves itself to be the true view by the fact that it combines the highest idealism, belief in the world-governing power of the deity with the common sense realism which sees the world as it actually is. The Christian's attitude to reality is always, to a certain extent, critical and polemical, because he measures it by his ideal, and he cannot overlook the distance between the reality and what ought to be. But with all this, for him it is not less firmly established that the world, in spite of all its imperfections, is the work of God, the object of the redeeming love, the place of the coming Kingdom. In this wonderful antinomy lies the enigma, lies the strength of Christianity."[1]

Pure theism states such an antinomy without hesitation, and is moreover able to suggest on which member of the antinomy the emphasis should be laid. It thus deepens in us a faith in the ultimate victory of the good, and the good which will be finally victorious is conceived as a good in which the value of each man's soul will be conserved and its sin and imperfection removed. It has been said that "man's vocation is in God or he has none". But this vocation is a call to eternal communion, the suggestion of a relation in which man and God shall continue as real personal factors, bound together in a unity of purpose, which purpose exists in the mind of God and will be gradually realised in the world through the united action of God and men. It is from such a faith alone that the moral force can come which is necessary for the overcoming of the evil that is in the world, and for deliverance from its sin. With such a faith we may be rendered secure in our optimism; without such a faith we are given over to pessimism of the most deadening and soul-destroying kind.

---

[1] *Philosophy and Development of Religion*, p. 314.

We have said that theism demands that God should be conceived of as both the source and end of the world. He is at the end what He was at the beginning, and thus He would seem to be out of time, and time would seem to have no real meaning for Him. On the other hand, we must think of God as entering into the world and working toward something not yet attained, sharing ideals with humanity and fighting along with them, in order that the ideas may be realised. It is the old difficulty of relating the eternal and the temporal, and a full statement of the relation is beyond human power. But more and more we are coming to lay stress on the reality of time, even as connected with God. God essentially enters into time in the creation of free personalities. From the original source there is an expansion of His being through the conditions He has laid upon Himself. God Himself develops as He differentiates Himself in the souls of men, and the consummation will be the completion of human personalities and the perfect harmony of them with God. So that, in the end, God will be all in all, having gained an infinite expansion through the human lives which, in working out *their own destiny*, discover that they also are divine.

But though this may be a vague hint of the ideal of theism, it may be questioned whether pure theism is sufficient to work out this ideal. Can theism do more than state the antinomy between the ideal and the actual, and suggest the direction in which the solution lies? Have we not described the process in too orderly a manner, and thus come dangerously near substituting a construction of thought for the actual process of development? In short, does pure theism deal adequately with the sin that is in the world, or consider sufficiently the weakness of the human heart? Can we work out our own destiny without assistance if we have, as it were, been entrusted only with the original endowment of freedom and self-determination? In committing the original trust to man, in deciding to create creators, God, if we may say it without irreverence, took certain risks, and in the course of development the seriousness of the risks have become very evident. Man received freedom of choice, but with this gift he also received the power of choosing evil rather than good. In face of the facts of the world we cannot deny that he exercised this power. We cannot deny the fact of sin, with all its consequent misery and gloom, which the Upanishads have so rightly emphasised. And often man has gone so far astray that the very power of return seems to have been taken from him. Was God to leave the matter thus? Would He provide no Redeemer?

We may return to the verse which has suggested the point of view of the last few pages—"God so loved the world that He sent His only begotten Son, that whosoever believeth in Him should not perish but have everlasting life." The love of God to the world is not merely the love which gives reality to the world, it is also the love which brings salvation. God has entrusted men with power which they often deliberately use to wander away from Him, but He does not leave them to these wanderings without a care for their fate. He will not recall the gift of freedom, but He retains the right to strengthen by additional bonds—or rather by more definite bonds—the connection between them and Himself. All down through the ages God has provided suggestions of the way in which men may return to Him, and this revelation of Himself, which the prophets brought to men, culminated in Christ when the fulness of time had come. Men had forgotten their divine origin and the world had become full of pain and evil. And so it was necessary that the love of God should manifest itself once more, and prove the divine more potent than all the pain and the sorrow and the evil. The divine love had to come to the rescue of human life, not in theory only but in fact. Christ came not to teach men how to think evil out of existence, but to show them how it could be conquered in the world and in their own lives; nay, more, He came to show them how it actually was conquered in the life of holiness and the death of sacrifice of the ideal man, who was also the Son of God. And, having been conquered in Christ and through Christ, evil could also be conquered in humanity. What was possible in Christ, the Elder Brother of the human race, might also be accomplished in His brethren of mankind. What He had won they might win, where He had gone there they might go. Sin was no longer an impossible barrier between them and God. Christ had taken upon Himself the burden of the sorrow of sin, and had returned through that sorrow to union with God, and in every human heart in which that divine sorrow should also be awakened, there might be peace and a consciousness of renewed communion with God. God was, in Christ, reconciling the world unto Himself. Through Christ the love of God streams forth to the utmost confines of humanity, giving to every man the power to return and become a son of God in the fullest sense, holding out the promise of an abundant life in complete harmony and unity with God.

Thus Christianity completes the teaching of the Upanishads. It is, like them, fully conscious of the sorrow and the evil of the world, but it finds salvation not in escape from the world but in victory over it, not in the destruction of the powers of humanity but in development of them, not in identity with and absorption in God but in communion and co-operation. Like the Upanishads, Christian thought seeks to attain to a conception of the Being of God, but it will not be satisfied with abstractions. If mere thought fails to give more than this, it will try other ways. It will supplement thought by feeling and devotion, and, taking human personality as its guide, it will continue in its search until it finds God also as a Person. But if the Christian is earnest in his search, he finds that he has not to go far in his own strength, God is also seeking for him and is drawing near to him in the person of the Eternal Son. God is no longer an abstract Being, far away in the dim distance. He is the Father of our Lord Jesus Christ, of whom the whole family in heaven and earth is named. So through the thunder comes a human voice, saying,

"O heart I made, a heart beats here!
Face, my hands fashioned, see it in myself!
Thou hast no power nor mayst conceive of mine,
But love I gave thee, with myself to love,
And thou must love me who have died for thee!"

With Christ, who thus has loved and ever loves humanity, a fulness of communion is possible which cannot be described by the intellect, but which may be experienced in heart and in life; and in the intensity with which the Christian mystic realises the presence of God he fulfils the ancient ideal of the Upanishads of the union of the Atman and Brahman. But he goes far beyond this ideal, for into the union of the Christian with God are brought all the riches of the being of both God and man. It is in the fulness of his humanity that man comes nearest God, and it is in the fulness of Divinity that God comes nearest man. The meeting-place is Christ. As in our search after God we retire from the world of our every-day into the mystery and the silence of our souls, we see the vision of the face of Christ and hear His voice, and, as we gaze more earnestly and listen more intently, we discover that we are looking upon the Face of God and hearkening to the voice of the Eternal.

"The worship of the impersonal laid no hold upon my heart," says the speaker in the *Ramayana* of Tulsidas. Christianity offers the worship of the personal, even the worship of the Christ, and He is laying hold of the heart of India.